A COURSE IN BUSINESS COMMUNICATION

Madhulika Jha
Shashi Shekhar

Orient BlackSwan

A Course in Business Communication

ORIENT BLACKSWAN PRIVATE LIMITED

Registered Office
3-6-752 Himayatnagar, Hyderabad 500 029 (A.P.), INDIA
e-mail: centraloffice@orientblackswan.com

Other Offices
Bangalore, Bhopal, Bhubaneshwar, Chennai, Ernakulam, Guwahati, Hyderbad, Jaipur, Kolkata, Lucknow, Mumbai, New Delhi, Patna

First published, 2010

ISBN 978 81 250 3990 7

Typeset in 11/13 pt Sabon

Typeset by
System Graphics (India) Pvt. Ltd.,
New Delhi

Printed in India at
Aadi Printech, Delhi

Published by
Orient Blackswan Private Limited
1/24 Asaf Ali Road
New Delhi 110 002
e-mail: delhi@orientblackswan.com

CONTENTS

INTRODUCTION

A Course in Business Communication focuses primarily on the communication needs of students pursuing business management courses. The book provides in-depth knowledge of the various forms and practices of business communication which should enable learners to understand the nuances of business communication and enhance their communication skills at the work place.

With the advent of new technology which has made the transfer of information a matter of fraction of seconds, it has become imperative for students of professional courses to acquire command over language. Learning to communicate in a manner that is clearly understood by the receiver of the message is a major task for all business people.

The focus is mostly on formal written communication because most official communication is done through writing. The structure of some technical documents and also the overall formation of a report need a specific format to be followed which is described through needed illustrations.

The book is developed as a learner-friendly manual where each chapter has a box at the beginning, informing readers about the learning outcomes of the chapter. At the end of each chapter are exercises based on the content, focusing on practical situations. The opening chapters of the book provide a detailed understanding of how effective communication is a professional advantage and how communication differs in different contexts and media. The aim of the book is to summarise the basic principles of communication and then to relate them to applications in formal situations. The coverage of business communication includes correspondence, report writing, and oral communication. At appropriate places, theory is related to specific applications.

Professionals in the fields of engineering and technology find it pertinent to communicate verbally as much as in writing. The book also contains chapters showing how one can give effective presentations. The primary approach while designing these chapters is to equip readers with effective tools for adequate information packaging and successful delivery. This helps in effectively planning, organising and delivering both short informal talks and long and mostly technical presentations. The book also deals with listening, and it is worth noting that the basis of the entire communication process is embedded in effective listening. Elimination of the barriers to efficient listening makes us more efficient communicators, while enabling other participants to do the same. As meetings are an integral part of official communication the book gives the reader guidelines on how to make meetings successful.

The aim of a successful student is to get himself/herself placed in an adequate position in a good organisation. This book also contains guidelines for enhancing employability by providing suggestions for creating effective resumes and handling interviews in an effective and positive manner. Today most communication is conducted through electronic media. A separate chapter is devoted to discuss the topic. It includes the different options available in e-mails and the correct way of sending e-mails along with the general etiquette to be followed while writing.

This book has incorporated in it the latest developments in the field of professional communication. The present compendium is an endeavour to offer the complex subject in a simple, coherent and comprehensive manner. We hope that students as well as teachers and professionals will find this book useful because of its preciseness and topics explicitly presented and discussed at length through sufficient illustrations.

Madhulika Jha
Shashi Shekhar

PART I

COMMUNICATION

Chapter 1

COMMUNICATION: ORIGIN AND SCOPE

Objectives

To introduce you to the

- Basic ideas of communication
- Types of communication
- Functions of communication
- Importance of communication

INTRODUCTION

This chapter will introduce you to the basic idea of communication, along with its types and functions. It will help you to understand the need for a clear and effective communication in an organisation, and will also help you to hone your communication skills. You will learn the communication process and its key elements.

The word communication is derived from the Latin word *comunicare*, which means 'to transmit'. The basic purpose of communication is to spread information, feelings, details and even knowledge to people around you. Good and effective communication is required not only for good human relations but also for good and successful business. Clear communication is not easy. The method, context, structure, language, knowledge and an understanding of the needs of the recipients to whom the information is being transmitted are vital in understanding the importance of communication in an organisation. Communication is one of the basic functions in any organisation. It is a process of transmitting information, ideas, thoughts, opinions and plans between various parts of an organisation.

FUNCTIONS OF EFFECTIVE COMMUNICATION

Communication skills are a set of skills that enable a person to clearly convey the relevant information to the required group or an individual. Listed below are various functions of effective communication:

It ensures that the members of an organisation know what is expected of them. For this correct information needs to be given to appropriate staff members.

Effective communication leads to good coordination between groups and individuals. Any kind of distortion or omission often leads to conflict, stress and misunderstanding between departments.

All the members of an organisation need to know about its plans and procedures. This leads to smooth functioning of the organisation.

THE COMMUNICATION PROCESS

Sender → Encoding→Channel→Decoding→Receiver ←Feedback

Encoding: The first step of the communication process is the encoding process. In order to convey meaning, the sender must begin encoding, which means packing information into a message in the form of symbols, language, gestures etc that represent ideas or concepts.

When encoding a message, the sender has to begin by deciding what needs to be transmitted. The sender has to keep in mind the receiver's knowledge and also keep into account the information that the receiver wants to know.

Channel: To begin transmitting the message, the sender uses some kind of channel (also called a medium). A channel could be oral or written, but these days visual channels are becoming more common because of technology. Some of the channels commonly used are telephone, e-mails, memos, letters, and reports. The effectiveness of the various channels fluctuates depending on the characteristics of the communication. For example, when immediate feedback is required, oral communication channels are more effective. When things are said to inform and need to be on record then written channels are preferred.

If the channel is not appropriate, the message could be confusing as well as it could be misunderstood by the receiver.

Decoding: After the appropriate channel or channels are selected, the message enters the decoding stage of the communication process. Decoding is carried on by the receiver. Once the message is received, the receiver examines it. He interprets the message and assigns a meaning to it. Successful communication takes place when the receiver correctly interprets the sender's message.

Feedback: Feedback is the final link in the chain of the communication process. After receiving a message, the receiver responds in some way to the sender. The signal may take the form of a spoken comment, a long sigh, a written message, a smile, or some other action. Feedback confirms that the receiver has received and interpreted the message correctly. It is therefore an essential component of the communication process. If there is a discrepancy in the feedback then it gives an opportunity to the sender to rectify or clarify his message.

BARRIERS TO EFFECTIVE COMMUNICATION

Communication cannot take place if there are barriers to the communication process. These must be recognised and removed.

Communication can often be improved by identifying the appropriate media. Written, verbal or electronic methods take time to deliver, while impersonal, are fast and can be effective. Meetings, interviews and video conferencing require personal, face to face communication and thus interpersonal skills. Telephone and public address systems should be used only where personal communication methods are difficult. Written communication is very often the most suitable and clearest means of communication and can take many forms: memoranda; occasional or annual reports (fundamental in communicating accounting information); forms; notices; house journals and other forms of standard documentation such as rules and procedures, manuals and job descriptions.

Visual communication is a powerful communication media and is often overlooked. Charts, slides, videos or films provide an immediate and clear message. Electronic means of communication are increasingly becoming more relevant. Document imaging, telex, fax, the Internet and e-mail are instantaneous and provide clear and fast communication possibilities.

The type of communication and the medium used will depend to a greater or lesser extent on organisational structure. This will in turn be a function of the product or service and its environment. There are many forms of communication within an organisation, formal and informal. Generally, in formal organisations information flows through quite clear channels and in defined directions. Traditionally, the direction of the three main information flows is downward, upward and lateral.

Downward communication is associated with giving orders or instructions from senior management. This form of communication is often the one most easily recognised. Its purpose is to give direction, goals, procedures and important notices. This helps the staff to know about the decisions of the seniors and the management.

Upward communication is communication that flows from the staff to the seniors. It generally consists of personal problems, suggestions and technical feedback.

Lateral or Horizontal communication is the most important kind. It is the communication that takes place between colleagues such as meetings. It helps in task coordination, resolving conflicts and even sharing ideas.

THE IMPORTANCE OF COMMUNICATION

Effective communication is an essential component of the business environment as there is a constant flow of information. For instance, a manager cannot get work done from his subordinates unless he communicates clearly what he wants to be done. He should also be sure of some basic facts such as how to communicate and what results should be expected from that communication. Most management problems arise because of lack of effective communication. Chances of misunderstanding and misrepresentation can be minimised with the help of a proper communication system.

Communication is also a basic tool for motivation, which helps in improving the morale of the employees. Inappropriate or faulty communication among employees or between the manager and his subordinates could be the major cause of conflict and low morale at work. A manager from time-to-time needs to tell his subordinates about how well they are doing and what more can be done.

With effective communication, you can maintain a good human relationship in the organisation and by encouraging ideas or suggestions from employees or workers and implementing them whenever possible, you can also increase production at low cost.

It is through the communication that employees submit their work reports, comments, grievances and suggestions to their seniors or management. Organisations should have an effective and speedy communication policy and procedures to avoid delays, misunderstandings, confusion or distortions of facts and to establish harmony among all the concerned people and departments.

So, effective communication is very important for successful working of an organisation.

TYPES OF COMMUNICATION

Procedural Communication

Procedural communication refers to the language and numeracy related to carrying out a task or a number of tasks. It includes giving instructions, applying and following a number of steps or procedures in order to perform and complete a task/s.

Technical Communication

Technical communication refers to the language and numeracy related to the use of tools or machines—whether simple or complex. It includes the language and mathematics involved in understanding and learning about media as well as about the function of technology and how to use it.

Personal Communication

Personal communication refers to the language and numeracy related to expressing personal identity and/or goals. It includes the different ways personal history, knowledge, attributes, goals and opinions are drawn on and expressed for particular purposes. It also includes the application of mathematics for individual needs such as personal finances or personal measurement.

Cooperative Communication

Cooperative communication refers to the language and numeracy related to understanding the function of a group and the roles of the different members, as well as to participating in the group including establishing cooperative relationships with its members.

Systems Communication

Systems communication refers to the language and numeracy related to understanding and interacting within an organisation or institution. In an educational institution or programme it includes learning about the range and design of educational choices and pathways as well as the relationship between classroom and non-classroom activities. It also involves the application of mathematics in or for institutional purposes.

Public Communication

Public communication refers to the language and numeracy related to understanding and interacting within the wider social or community context. In an educational institution or programme it includes learning about and interacting with other institutions—educational ones, those in local community or those related to employment—for the purposes of future work or study, entertainment or engagement with public interest issues. It also involves the application of mathematics in or for a public context or need.

NONVERBAL AND VERBAL COMMUNICATION

Non-verbal Communication

Nonverbal Communication (NVC) is sending and receiving wordless messages. Such messages can be communicated through gesture; body language or posture; facial expression and eye contact; object communication such as clothing, hairstyles or even architecture; symbols and graphics. Speech may also contain nonverbal elements known as paralanguage, which includes voice quality, emotion and speaking style, as well as prosodic features such as rhythm, intonation and stress. Likewise, written texts have nonverbal elements such as handwriting style, spatial arrangement of words, or the use of emotions.

Written Communication

Communication can be oral or written. In oral communication, listeners can make out what the speaker is saying, but in written communication, text matter in the message is a reflection of the communicator's thinking. So, written communication or message should be clear, purposeful and concise with correct words, to avoid any misinterpretation. Written communications provides a permanent record; and therefore needs to be drafted properly.

Verbal communication includes sounds, spoken words and language. Some of the examples of verbal communication are telephone conversations, meetings, presentations, public speaking, etc.

However, vocal sounds that are not considered to be words, such as a grunt, or singing a wordless note, are nonverbal. Sign languages and writing are generally understood as forms of verbal communication, as both make use of words—although like speech, both may contain paralinguistic elements and often occur alongside nonverbal messages. Nonverbal communication can occur through any sensory channel—sight, sound, smell, touch or taste.

Proxemics

Proxemics is the study of how people use and perceive the physical space around them. It was developed by Edward T. Hall, who studied how animals showed territoriality. The space between the sender and the receiver of a message influences the way the message is interpreted.

The perception and use of space varies significantly across cultures and different settings within cultures. Space in nonverbal communication may be divided into four main categories: intimate, social, personal, and public space. The distance between communicators will also depend on sex, status, and social role.

Further, scholars have identified four territories:

Primary territory: An area that is associated with someone who exclusively uses it. Here you need the owner's permission to enter. For example, a house.

Secondary territory: Unlike the previous type, there is no 'right' to occupancy, but people may still feel some degree of ownership of this kind of space. For example, someone may sit in the same seat on the bus every day.

Public territory: An area that is available to all, but only for a set period, such as a parking space or a seat in a library.

Interaction territory: Space created by others when they are interacting. For example, when a bunch of people talking to each other they form a group wherever they are (in a mall, on footpath) will walk around the group rather than disturb it.

Chronemics

Chronemics is the study of the use of time in nonverbal communication. Time perceptions include punctuality and willingness to wait, the length of speech and how long people are willing to listen. All this contributes to the interpretation of nonverbal messages.

Kinesics

It is the study of body movements, facial expressions, and gestures. It was developed by anthropologist Ray L. Birdwhistell and it includes mutual gazing, smiling, facial warmth or pleasantness, childlike behaviours, direct body orientation, and the like.

Posture

Posture depicts a participant's degree of attention or involvement. Posture is understood through such indicators as direction of lean, body orientation, arm position, and body openness.

Studies suggest that mirror-image congruent postures, where one person's left side is parallel to the other's right side, leads to favourable perception of communicators and positive speech; a person who displays a forward lean or a decrease in a backward lean also shows a positive posture. A gesture is a non-vocal bodily movement intended to express meaning.

The boundary between language and gesture, or verbal and nonverbal communication, is difficult to identify.

Eye Gaze

The study of the role of eyes in nonverbal communication is sometimes referred to as 'occulics'. Eye contact can indicate interest, attention, and involvement. Gaze comprises the actions of looking while talking, looking while listening, amount of gaze, and frequency of glances, patterns of fixation, pupil dilation, and blink rate.

Paralanguage

Paralanguage (sometimes called vocalics) is the study of nonverbal cues of the voice. Various acoustic properties of speech such as tone, pitch and accent, collectively known as prosody, can all give off nonverbal cues. Paralanguage may change the meaning of words.

1. The *voice set* is the context in which the speaker is speaking. This can include the situation, gender, mood, age and a person's culture.
2. The *voice qualities* are volume, pitch, tempo, rhythm, articulation, resonance, nasality, and accent. They give each individual a unique 'voice print'.
3. *Vocalisation* consists of three sub-sections: characterisers, qualifiers and segregates. Characterisers are emotions expressed while speaking, such as laughing, crying, and yawning. A voice qualifier is the style of delivering a message—for example, yelling "Hey what are you doing?", as opposed to whispering "Hey, what are you doing?".

VERBAL COMMUNICATION

The communication mode which we rely on most often to carry meaning from one person to another is the verbal mode. One of the difficulties with words is that we attach to them different experiential and emotional connotations. Difficulties could arise in understanding what is being said if the speaker uses jargon, clichés, and the use of specialised vocabularies. Words usually have a meaning when they are associated with people in context.

It is not uncommon to observe people attempting to find the right words to say what they mean.

INTERACTION OF VERBAL AND NONVERBAL COMMUNICATION

When communicating, nonverbal messages can interact with verbal messages in six ways: repeating, conflicting, complementing, substituting, regulating and accenting/moderating.

Repeating

Repeating consists of using gestures to strengthen a verbal message, such as pointing to the object of discussion.

Conflicting

Verbal and nonverbal messages within the same interaction can sometimes send opposing or conflicting messages. A person verbally expressing a statement of truth while simultaneously fidgeting or avoiding eye contact may convey a mixed message to the receiver in the interaction. Conflicting messages may occur for a variety of reasons often stemming from feelings of uncertainty, ambivalence, or frustration. When mixed messages occur, nonverbal communication becomes the primary tool people use to attain additional information to clarify the situation; great attention is placed on bodily movements and positioning when people perceive mixed messages during interactions.

Complementing

Accurate interpretation of messages is made easier when nonverbal and verbal communication complement each other. Nonverbal cues can be used to elaborate on verbal messages to reinforce the information sent when trying to achieve communicative goals; messages have been shown to be remembered better when nonverbal signals affirm the verbal exchange.

Substituting

Nonverbal behaviour is sometimes used as the sole channel for communication of a message. People learn to identify facial expressions, body movements, and body positioning as corresponding with specific feelings and intentions. Nonverbal signals can be used without verbal communication to convey messages; when nonverbal behaviour does not effectively communicate a message, verbal methods are used to enhance understanding.

Regulating

Nonverbal behaviour also regulates our conversations. For example, touching someone's arm can signal that you want to talk next or interrupt.

Accenting/Moderating

Nonverbal signals are used to alter the interpretation of verbal messages. Touch, voice pitch, and gestures are some of the tools people use to accent or amplify the message that is sent; nonverbal behaviour can also be used to moderate or tone down aspects of verbal messages as well. For example, a person who is verbally expressing anger may accent the verbal message by shaking a fist.

Conclusion

These two modes of communication—verbal and nonverbal—are used by every person. Nonverbal signals and cues are continuous, as we, voluntarily or involuntarily, give out a continuous string of messages to other people. Those messages, of course, may be different from what we intend. There is also the possibility that our intentions are not highly correlated with our actual gut-level experience. When we are awake and talking with each other, we are giving out three sets of signals. These signals may not be correlated with each other. Our tongues may be saying one thing, our bodies saying another thing, and our appearance may be saying a third thing. True communication results when people share a common meaning experience. If there is a consistency among the cues that one is using to share meaning, then communication is much more likely to occur. When one is saying one thing and experiencing another, then he/she is giving out mixed signals that can be very misleading and confusing to the other person.

For communication to occur, there must be a two-way interchange of feelings, ideals and values. One-way communication is highly inefficient in that there is no way to determine whether what is heard is what is intended. The office memo is a form of one-way communication which is perhaps the least effective medium for transmitting meaning. A second implication is that for true communication to be experienced, it is necessary that there be a feedback process inherent in the communication effort. There needs to be a continuous flow back and forth among the people attempting to communicate, sharing what they heard from each other. The third implication is that the individual person needs to become acutely aware of the range of signals which they are emitting at any given moment. They can learn that by soliciting feedback from the people with whom they are attempting to share meaning.

ASSIGNMENT

1. What are the functions of effective communication?
2. Briefly describe the communication process?

3. What are the barriers to effective communication? How should they be resolved?
4. Briefly describe verbal and nonverbal communication.

Chapter 2

PRESENTATION SKILLS

Objectives

To enable you to:

- Plan, develop, and deliver presentations
- Learn how to assess and engage with your audience
- Understand the important elements of a presentation
- Answer the questions of the audience

INTRODUCTION

Management is the art of getting things done. A presentation is a fast and potentially effective method of getting things done through other people. In managing any project, presentations are used as a formal method for bringing people together to plan, monitor and review its progress.

BENEFITS OF PRESENTATIONS

1. There are members of your organisation who need to know about your projects. They could be your subordinates, who need to assist you with it, or senior management who might want to know the pace of progress of your work. Presentations display the required information to them. It helps them in taking decisions and also helps them raise queries.
2. It helps to put forth issues, problems and loopholes to the relevant audience. This leads to discussions which eventually find solutions to the problem presented.
3. Presentations also help to display your product to clients/customers. It helps dispersing relevant information about it.

Objectives of Presentation

The single most important observation is that the objective of communication is not the transmission but the reception. The whole preparation, presentation and content of a speech must therefore be geared not to the speaker but to the audience. The presentation of a perfect project plan is a failure if the audience does not understand or are not persuaded of its merits The objective of communication is to make your message understood and remembered. A presentation should:

1. Make the audience understand the purpose of your presentation.
2. Be gripping enough to hold the attention of the audience.
3. Convince the audience about your venture.
4. Clearly present the facts and figures which would facilitate decision making.

HOW TO PREPARE A PRESENTATION

Plan

A presenter should plan what she wants to put forward in the presentation. The presenter must concentrate not only upon the facts being presented but upon the style, pace, tone and ultimately tactics which should be used too.

Formulate your Objectives

It is very important to formulate a precise objective. This should take the form of a simple, concise statement of intent. For example, the purpose of your speech may be to obtain funds, to evaluate a proposal, or to motivate your team. If you do not focus upon your objective, it is unlikely that the audience will understand your point.

Identify the Audience

The next task is to identify your audience. Essentially this is done by identifying their aims and objectives while attending to your presentation. If you can somehow convince them they are achieving those aims while at the same time achieving your own, you will find a helpful and receptive audience. For instance, if you are seeking approval for a new product plan from the senior management, it is useful to know and understand their main objectives. If they are currently worried that their product range, you could emphasise how your new product would increase the product range. You have to address their problem at the very beginning, and inform them that your presentation has solutions to their problems. This will make them more attentive.

Structure

Present your thoughts in a structured manner, keeping in mind the main message. Your speech should have a proper structure otherwise the audience will not be able to follow you. Having established the aim of your presentation you should choose the most appropriate structure to achieve it.

The Beginning

It is imperative to plan your beginning carefully; there are six main elements that you need to keep in mind.

Get their attention

You have to grab their attention at the very beginning. You could do this by addressing the issues that are bothering them.

Establish a theme

Basically, you need to start the audience thinking about the subject matter of your presentation. This can be done by a statement of your main objective. They will each have some experience or opinions on this and at the beginning you must make them bring that experience into their own minds.

Present a structure

If you explain briefly at the beginning of a talk how it is to proceed, then the audience will know what to expect. This can help to establish the theme and also provide something concrete to hold their attention. Ultimately, it provides a sense of security in the promise that this speech too will end.

Create a rapport

If you can win the audience over in the first minute, you will keep them for the remainder. You should plan exactly how you wish to appear to them and use the beginning to establish that relationship. You may be presenting yourself as their friend, as an expert, perhaps even as a judge, but whatever role you choose you must establish it at the very beginning.

Administration

When planning your speech you should make a note to find out if there are any administrative details which need to be announced at the beginning of your speech. This is not simply to make yourself popular with the people organising the session but also because if these details are over looked, the audience may become distracted as they wonder what is going to happen next.

The Ending

The final impression you make on the audience is the one they will remember. Thus it is worth planning your last few sentences with extreme care.

Visual Aids

Most people expect visual reinforcement for any verbal message being delivered. You can use a projector, a slide show, or even a video presentation. These visual aids are a very crucial part of any presentation. You could give graphs or pie charts to compare facts and figures. The audience will grasp the point faster with the help of visual aids.

The Delivery

Your job as a manager is to use the potential of the presentation to ensure that the audience is motivated and inspired rather than disconcerted or distracted. There are five key facets of the human body which deserve attention in presentation skills: the eyes, the voice, the expression, the appearance, and how you stand.

The Eyes

It is important to maintain eye contact with your audience. This results into assurance and also builds a rapport.

The Voice

A monotone speech is both boring and soporific, so it is important to try to vary the pitch and speed of your presentation. At the very least, each new sub-section should be preceded by a pause and a change in tone to emphasis the delineation. If tonal variation does not come to you naturally try making use of rhetorical questions throughout your speech.

Expression

Keep your facial expressions as natural as you can. Don't show your nervousness and keep calm.

Appearance

There are many guides to management and presentation styles which lay heavy emphasis upon the way you dress and in the last analysis this is a matter of personal choice. That choice should however be deliberately made. When you are giving a presentation you must dress for the audience, not for yourself; if they think you look out of place, then you are. However, you have to dress up formally.

Stance

You must do is make sure that the way you stand does not convey boredom; at best, you can use your whole body as a dynamic tool to reinforce your rapport with the audience.

The perennial problem is what to do with your hands. These must not wave aimlessly through the air, or fiddle constantly with a pen, or (worst of all visually) juggle change in your trouser pockets. The key is to keep your hands still, except when used in accord with your speech.

Elements of a Presentation

Content It should contain information that people need. But unlike reports, which are read at the reader's own pace, presentations must account for how much information the audience can absorb in one sitting.

Structure It should have a logical beginning, middle, and end. It must be sequenced and paced so that the audience can understand it. Whereas reports have appendices and footnotes to guide the reader, the speaker must be careful not to loose the audience when wandering from the main point of the presentation.

Packaging It must be well prepared. A report can be reread and portions skipped over, but this is not the case here.

Human Element A good presentation will be remembered much more than a good report because it has a person attached to it. But you still need to analyse if the audience's needs would not be better met if a report was sent instead.

The Voice The voice is probably the most valuable tool of the presenter. It carries most of the content that the audience takes away. One of the oddities of speech is that we can easily tell others what is wrong with their voice, e.g. too fast, too high, too soft, etc., but we have trouble listening to and changing our own voices. Maintain proper volume, tone and pitch.

The Body Your body communicates different impressions to the audience. People not only listen to you, they also watch you. Therefore maintain a good posture.

Questions A presentation is always followed by questions. Sometimes questions could be raised while you give your presentation too. Understand the question and give a clear answer. Keep cool if a questioner disagrees with you.

Remember, questions do not mean you did not explain the topic well enough, but that their interest is deeper than that of the average audience.

Always allow time at the end of the presentation for questions. After inviting questions, do not rush ahead if no one asks a question. Pause for about 6 seconds to allow the audience to gather their thoughts. When a question is asked, repeat the question to ensure that everyone heard it (and that you heard it correctly). When answering, direct your remarks to the entire audience. That way, you keep everyone focused, not just the questioner. To reinforce your presentation, try to relate the question back to the main points.

Make sure you listen to the question being asked. If you do not understand it, ask them to clarify. Pause to think about the question as the answer you give may be correct, but ignore the main issue. If you do not know the answer, be honest and do not waffle. Be precise while answering questions. Do not make your answers too lengthy.

ASSIGNMENT

1. Discuss in detail the elements of a good presentation.
2. What qualities does a good speaker possess?
3. How are visual aids important in a presentation?
4. What points do you need to take into consideration while preparing a presentation?

Chapter 3

NEGOTIATION SKILLS

Objectives

To enable you to:

- Understand the negotiation process
- How to plan and prepare for negotiation
- To understand the importance of negotiation and how to use it effectively

INTRODUCTION

Negotiation skills are an interpersonal or an inter-group process, where the participants discuss and finally agree on a solution to their problems or resolve a dispute between them. They search for a solution that suits all the parties that are negotiating. These are usually inter-dependent and have interlocking goals. The degree of their interdependence has a major impact on the negotiation, the way it is conducted and its outcomes. It is the primary method of alternative dispute resolution.

The disputants, while negotiating, either attempt to force the other side to comply with their demands, to modify the opposing position and move toward compromise, or to invent a solution that meets the objectives of all sides.

Mutual adjustment is one of the key causes of the changes that occur during a negotiation. Both parties know that they can influence the other's outcomes and that the other side can influence theirs. The effective negotiator attempts to understand how people will adjust and readjust their positions during negotiations, based on what the other party does and is expected to do. The parties have to exchange information and make an effort to influence each other. As negotiations evolve, each side proposes changes to the other party's position and makes changes to its own. This process of give-and-take and making concessions is necessary if a settlement is to be reached. If one party makes several proposals that are rejected, and the other party makes no alternate proposal, the first party may break off negotiations. Parties typically will not want to concede too much if they do not sense that those with whom they are negotiating are willing to compromise.

The parties must work toward a solution that takes into account each person's requirements and hopefully optimises the outcomes for both. As they try to find their way towards an agreement, the parties focus on interests, issues, and positions, and use cooperative and/or competitive processes to come to an agreement.

Negotiation occurs in business, non-profit organisations, government branches, legal proceedings, among nations and in everyday life.

Effective negotiation helps you to resolve situations where what you want conflicts with what someone else wants. The aim of negotiation is to find a solution that is acceptable to both parties.

PREPARATION FOR NEGOTIATION

Depending on the scale of the disagreement, some preparation may be appropriate for conducting a successful negotiation. If you need to resolve a major disagreement, then make sure you prepare thoroughly. Go through the following points before you start negotiating:

- *Goals:* It's important to know what you want to get out of the negotiation. Without an appropriate goal, your negotiation will be aimless and hence useless.
- *Trades:* As negotiation is about giving and taking you should have a clear picture in your mind about the kind of compromises you would be comfortable making.
- *Alternatives:* If you don't reach agreement with the other person, what alternatives do you have? These alternatives give you a sense of security.
- *Relationships:* Keep in mind the kind of impact the negotiation will have on your relationship with the other party.
- *Expected outcomes:* What outcome will people be expecting from this negotiation? What has the outcome been in the past, and what precedents have been set?
- *The consequences:* What are the consequences for you of winning or losing this negotiation? What are the consequences for the other person?
- *Possible solutions:* Think about all the possible solutions and discuss them with the other party while negotiating.

IMPACTS OF NEGOTIATION

For a negotiation to be 'win-win', both parties should feel positive about the negotiation once it is over. This helps people keep a good working relationship afterwards.

The negotiation itself is a careful exploration of your position and the other person's position, with the goal of finding a mutually acceptable compromise that gives you both as much of what you want as possible. People's positions are rarely as fundamentally opposed as they may initially appear—the other person may have very different goals.

In an ideal situation, you will find that the other person wants what you are prepared to trade, and that you are prepared to give what the other person wants.Ultimately, both sides should feel comfortable with the final solution if the agreement is to be considered win-win.

Only consider win-lose negotiation if you don't need to have an ongoing relationship with the other party as, having lost, they are unlikely to want to work with you again. Equally, you should expect that if they need to fulfill some part of a deal in which you have 'won', they may be uncooperative and legalistic about the way they do this.

THE PROCESS OF NEGOTIATION

Negotiation is a process involving two or more people of either equal or unequal power, meeting to discuss shared and/or opposed interests in relation to a particular area of mutual concern.

As a process, negotiation has three dimensions. First, negotiation is an educational process: it enlightens the other side about your team's concerns, perceptions and aspirations. Second, negotiation is a problem-solving process: inevitably the parties involved have different perspectives that must be reconciled if there is to be progress. Third, negotiation is an interdependent process: workable and sustainable progress depends on building a cooperative relationship with the other side. In general, negotiating a workable balance among competing interests requires a combination of direct and indirect diplomacy, discussion and consultation, compromise and concession, and above all, flexibility.

Moreover, negotiation is about 'conflict'. In negotiation, conflict tends to be a product of the different interests held by the parties in relation to the area under discussion. The nature of the conflict is conditioned by the substantive, psychological and procedural requirements of both sides: respectively, the minimum objective, emotional needs, and resolution and implementation procedures requiring satisfaction for there to be an agreement. The conflict therefore need not be destructive: it can be used to promote communication and discussion which allows the parties to redefine old, unworkable, or to establish new, relationships. Furthermore, the nature of conflict changes over time which allows new opportunities for discussion and reconciliation. In general it is important to understand the nature of the conflict and to legitimise it in the negotiating process.

Finally, negotiation is about power. Power is the capacity to realise a desired outcome, or to change the stance of another party. Negotiation inevitably involves parties with different capabilities and resources. The ability to utilise these differences in an effective exercise of power will depend on the political, economic and social context surrounding the negotiations. The exercise of power manifests itself in the words and phrases used in the final agreement. It is therefore a contingent phenomenon subject to the particularities of the situation and the abilities of the parties involved to function in the given negotiating environment. As a result, in a contest of wills it is not inevitable that the party with greater resources and influence will always realise its objectives. In general, negotiating a workable solution among competing interests requires an understanding of the power dynamics at work because these will set the parameters in which an agreement will be realised.

Most of the negotiation literature focuses on two strategies, although they call them by different names. One strategy is interest-based (or integrative, or cooperative) bargaining, while the other is positional (or distributive or competitive) bargaining.

You have to remember the following points while negotiating:

- You have to try and find a common ground.
- Seek to understand the other party's position/situation. Explain yours.
- Active listening is critical.
- Exploring Differences

Objectives

- Understand goals of negotiation
- Recognise negotiator roles and reasons for behaviour
- Improve preparatory skills
- Understand and practice the negotiation process

Why Negotiate?

- Gain greater understanding of the other side's motives, objectives, and constraints
- Allow the other side to learn some of your motives, objectives, constraints
- Seek common ground

This is the crux of the issue. The goal of negotiation is mutual success of both parties in meeting their needs. It is contrasted with competition, in which one side wins, the other loses.

- Build relationships

You may want or need to enter into future negotiations with the same or related parties. Building a good relationship facilitates effective future negotiations.

When to Negotiate?

- Win-win outcome is desirable to both parties
- You occupy a defensible position
- Your offer/counteroffer should make sense, and be supportable with facts.
- You have options
- The other side has options

Both sides must have some room to, or else you're dealing with an ultimatum: "Take it or leave it."

When to NOT Negotiate

- You are in competition with the other party.
- One or both sides enter with false intentions (both sides must want win/win).
- You can't possibly win.
- You or other party lack authority to make commitments.

Negotiator Roles

- Equal parties
- Employer/Employee
- Superior/Subordinate
- Agent/Beneficiary (or other recipient)
- Seller/Customer

You may occupy any or all of these roles at various times in your career.

Your role determines

- What latitude you have
- What behaviour expected of you
- Behaviour you expect from other side
- Constraints

Preparing to Negotiate

- Determine roles.
- Examine your position.
- Strengths, weaknesses
- Limits, and ranges of options

For each issue, you need to determine your minimum acceptable value, your best-possible (realistic) value, and your target value, somewhere between the first two.

- Consider the other party's needs.
- How would you proceed in their role?
- Identify and prioritise key issues, and set goals and strategies.

Decide before hand what your negotiation ranges are for each of your issues, and which issues are most important. Concentrate on getting at least your target values on the most important issues. That allows you more flexibility with the less important issues. Develop your justifications for the most important issues.

- Work through emotions beforehand.

Strive to remain calm, diplomatic, and principled throughout, no matter what the other side does or says. Anticipate problem areas. Never resort to attacking the other party or third parties. It simply doesn't work!

ASSIGNMENT

1. Discuss the negotiation process in detail.
2. What are the impacts of negotiation?
3. What is negotiation? Discuss its objectives.
4. What points does one need to keep in mind before negotiating?

Chapter 4

MEETINGS

Objectives

To enable you to:

- To learn the benefits of a meeting
- To understand the process of a meeting
- To enable you to organise a meeting

INTRODUCTION

Meetings are an important part of corporate life today. In a meeting, two or more people come together to discuss a predetermined topic often in a formal setting. Meetings also serve as vehicles for individual advancement and organisational achievement. Successful, constructive meetings take place as a result of careful preparation. When preparing for meeting keep these crucial aims in mind

KINDS OF MEETINGS

Recurring meeting: It is a meeting that recurs periodically, such as a weekly staff meeting. The meeting organiser wants the participants to be at the meeting on a constant and repetitive basis.

Series meeting: It is like a recurring meeting, but the details differ from meeting to meeting. The place where it is held is the same but the agenda and topics vary.

Status Meetings: These meetings are generally Leader-led, which are about reporting by one-way communication.

Work Meetings: These are meetings which produce a product or intangible result such as a decision.

Staff meeting: This is a meeting between a manager and his subordinates.

Team meeting: A meeting among colleagues working on various aspects of a team project.

Ad- hoc meeting: It is a meeting which is called for a special purpose.

Management meeting: A meeting among senior managers.

Board meeting: A meeting where Board of Directors discuss about company's policies, strategies, and growth.

One-on-one meeting: A meeting between two individuals.

PURPOSES

Every meeting is called for a purpose and it is this purpose which gives form to the meeting. The purpose of the meeting can be either informational or decision making.

Meetings for informational purposes:

- To communicate important or sensitive information
- To explore new ideas and concepts
- To provide feedback
- To gain for an idea, or project
- To present a report

An informational meeting is that where the participants can share information and possibly coordinate actions. This involves individual briefings by each participant or a speech by the leader followed by questions from the participants.

Decision making meetings are mainly concerned with persuasions, analysis and problem solving. They often include a brainstorming which is followed by a debate on the alternatives.

Meetings for decision making purposes:

- To reach a group decision.
- To solve a problem
- To reconcile a conflict.
- To negotiate an agreement
- To win acceptance for new ideas.

Meetings can serve many other legitimate purposes. For instance, they are used to build morale, plan projects or strategies, and also to provide training to employees, suppliers or customers.

THE ROLE OF A CHAIRPERSON

In a meeting, the chairperson plays three primary roles of leader, facilitator and participant.

There are certain responsibilities a chairperson should hold in order to make the meeting very effective:

1. Getting the meeting off to a good start
2. Encouraging the participants to participate in the meeting
3. Joining the discussion
4. Managing the emotions
5. Dealing with the late comers
6. Managing conflict
7. Injecting humour
8. Ending the meeting

When all the items in the agenda have been covered the meeting comes to an end whether or not the scheduled time has run out.

In closing the meeting, the leader should sum up what has been accomplished and what remains to be done. If another meeting is to be held the leader should set the tentative time and date for the meeting.

After the meeting is over the secretary needs to work on the minutes of the meeting.

ELEMENTS OF A MEETING

Agenda

A written agenda is the list of the individual items that need to be discussed in the meeting. In business meetings, the agenda may also be known as the *orders of the day*. The agenda is usually distributed to the participants prior to the meeting, so that they are aware of the subjects to be discussed, and are able to prepare for the meeting accordingly.

With the objectives defined you can begin to develop an agenda, keeping the following guidelines in mind:

1. *Number of agenda items:* Focus on a few critical items. Limiting the agenda items leads to an effective meeting. It is very essential to arrange the items in a logical and a coherent manner for an effective meeting.
2. *Include sufficient details:* An agenda item should give the participants the specific information they need to prepare for the meeting. It should enable them to understand the main purpose of the meeting.

   Include the following details in your agenda-

   a. Name of the organisation and department.
   b. Date, time and venue.
   c. Items to be discussed.

Minutes

Minutes are a record of what happened at a meeting. They serve as a useful tool to remind the participants what actions they need to take as a result of the discussion, show the process of arriving at certain decision and also serve as a repository of information for future reference. They often give an overview of the structure of the meeting, starting with a list of those present, a statement of the various issues before the participants, and each of their responses thereto. They could be written/typed notes or even recorded. They serve as a crucial official document.

ASSIGNMENT

1. What is an agenda? Discuss its importance.
2. Discuss the importance of minutes of a meeting.
3. Why are meetings a crucial part of the business world?
4. Discuss the role of a chairperson.

PART I I

ORAL COMMUNICATION

Chapter 5

SPEAKING SKILLS

Objectives

To introduce you to:

- Kinds of speaking skills
- Effective ways of speaking
- Public speaking

INTRODUCTION

Communication is a process of sending and receiving information which leads to exchange of information. Oral communication describes any kind of interaction that makes use of spoken words or actions. It is an integral part of the business world. Information cannot be effectively received, transferred or exchanged without using good communication skills. There are two kinds of skills in oral communication:

1. Speaking
2. Listening

In this and the next chapter we are going to discuss these two skills in detail.

Speaking is an art and plays a vital role in our everyday life. A good speaker is a person who can deliver an effective dialogue, which lucidly expresses their ideas, thoughts, and feelings. Some of the key components of verbal communication are sound, words, speech, and language.

SPEAKING SKILLS

Speaking skills, like other language skills are more complicated than it seems and involves much more than sending out a volley of words and it remains one of the most basic functions of our lives. We communicate with our fellow beings in a variety of ways and it is important to develop one's speaking skills in order to communicate more effectively. It is important to focus on our speech and therefore develop the requisite speaking skills, which include, among other things

- Tonality
- Expression
- Emphasis

In order to do so, one must develop the micro-skills of speaking and there should be clarity of both thought and diction in what we want to convey. Here are some of the micro-skills involved in speaking:

- Clarity in pronunciation, so that the hearer can distinguish the distinctive sounds. Mispronunciation can often lead to embarrassments.
- Correct use of stress and rhythmic patterns of the language. For example in English, wh-questions have a rising tone.
- Correct grammar and vocabulary. Special attention should be paid to tense and gender.
- Correct use of register or language that is appropriate to the situation and the audience.

When communicating in diverse situations, it is important to know how to respond to the situation through our speaking skills. There are three kinds of speaking situations in which we find ourselves.

- Interactive
- Partially interactive
- Non-interactive

Among them, the one that we frequently come across is the interactive situation. It includes face-to-face conversations with individuals or a small, group, greetings and telephone calls, where we are alternatively listening and speaking and where we have a chance to ask for clarification, or repetition from our conversation partner. A partially interactive situation is when we are addressing a large audience present in front of us. Though it is not customary for the audience to interrupt the speech, we can judge their response from the expression on their faces, or their body language, which is known as non-verbal communication.

A non-interactive speaking situation is when we are electronically recording a speech, say for a video or a radio or television speech, where there is no interaction with the conversation partner/audience.

Speaking forms an integral part of oral communication and possessing solid oratory skills is vital in any business environment. Your linguistic abilities, combined with your body language and mannerism showcase your business acumen. As a company's representative, both customers and colleagues alike will be attracted to someone who can effectively and succinctly exchange messages. If people feel they cannot communicate with you, this may cause conflict in the work environment.

Two main areas where managers require verbal communication are: interpersonal and public speaking. As majority of speaking is an interpersonal process, in order to communicate effectively we also need to form a rapport with the people.

Interpersonal Communication

Communication in the work place comes in many forms and the most common one is conversation with one's subordinates, peers and seniors or even with people outside the organisation. Talking does not unilaterally mean that we are able to convey our message. Something might get lost in the middle if we are insensitive to our conversation partner and are unable to draw them into the conversation. Our body language, facial and tonal expressions should not send out signals that are contrary to what we are trying to convey. While in any kind of conversation you either express your viewpoint—agreeing or disagreeing with your conversation partner over something inconsequential; the difference in a business conversation is that it is an interaction with a purpose. Your success lies in how much you are able to convince your conversation partner about what you are saying.

Public speaking

Public speaking is an art of presenting an idea or service to an audience. As a business manager you may be asked to make a presentation to your colleagues, your seniors, clients or the general public. Depending on the audience, your focus on the topic and your manner of presentation will be different. However, regardless of the audience, the subject or the duration of the talk, you will be expected to communicate effectively with your audience and engage with them directly. If you are making a presentation or delivering a lecture, you need to plan it ahead and below are some points which you need to remember.

- *The audience:* Whenever you are asked to make a speech or presentation, you will be told whom you will have to address and it is very important for you to understand your audience. For example, if you are asked to speak to some new recruits at an induction programme, you will realise that your audience knows very little about the organisation they have just joined, and the onus will be on you to give them a clear picture about the organisation, its expectations from its employees as well as their expectations from the organisation. On the other hand, if you are selling a product or service to a client, you are likely to stress on the quality of the product and the benefits the client will get from this product or service provided. In this instance you are unlikely to talk about your organisation, except in terms of the service they are able to provide. So it is always best if you know your audience in advance and the expectations they might have of you.
- *The subject:* When you are addressing an audience, it is but natural that they have some expectations from you. So, once you have determined your audience and know

what you are going to speak about, plan the way you want to make the presentation. Read up on the subject and be prepared to take questions. Also decide how you want to make the presentation. This we will discuss in detail below.

- How to deliver presentations and proposals
  - Impromptu speech
  - Speaking from memory
  - Reading from a manuscript
  - Using visual aids

Impromptu speech

An impromptu speech is perhaps the most difficult kind of public speaking as you do not get enough time to prepare yourself. It could arise out of an unforeseen demand or when you have to firefight for your team. In most business situations you will be expected to speak on a topic within your range of experience, so you should not feel nervous but speak up to the audience.

Speaking from memory

It is best to train yourself to speak from memory rather than try and memorise your speech as you are likely to forget lines and fumble. You can make small notes and use them as props to help you along in your speech.

Reading from a manuscript

Some business presentations such as Annual Reports or technical reports require to be read out. Try and modulate your voice and articulate yourself so that you are able to get through to your audience. As you are reading out from a manuscript, you are likely to have less eye contact with your audience, so pause to gage their reactions.

Using visual aids

Your audience is likely to remember your presentation, if it is enhanced with visuals. The most common way of presenting visual aids is using a Power Point Presentation (PPT). Graphics like pie charts, tables, figure, etc can be shown very effectively. However, when you are making the presentation, please keep in mind that the graphics should be very clear and visible even to the person sitting in the last row. For visuals like graphs or pie charts, see that you use colour coding that is distinct so that different areas that you shade are not similar in colour. Also ensure that whatever you say is in sync with the visuals.

Characteristics of an effective speaker

- Use simple, jargon-free language, unless the audience is specialised in the subject area.

- Make sure you complete your sentences.
- Do not speak too fast. Give audience time to register what you are saying.
- In interpersonal speaking, etiquette is very important.
- To be an ȇffective communicator one must speak in a manner that is not offending to the receiver.

SMALL TALK

Small talk is an informal kind of discourse that comments on what is perfectly obvious. It is conversation for its own sake. It can be a very relevant source of exchange of information in both formal and informal settings. It is a conversation that usually melts the discomfort and awkwardness between two strangers. It comes before a drawn out conversation or is just a small conversation in itself. The possibilities for small talks are:

At the Beginning of a Conversation

When two people begin to talk about a certain issue, they initially engage themselves in small talk, which forms a certain kind of rapport between them. They are also able to sense each other's mood.

At the End of a Conversation

Small talk at the end of the conversation helps to give a positive note to the relationship between people, and it also softens the parting.

As a space filler

Silence between two strangers often makes them uncomfortable. Talking reduces this discomfort and leads to healthy discussion later. Given below are some common topics that you can safely base small talk on:

1. Sports
2. Hobbies
3. Weather
4. Family
5. Movies and Television
6. Holidays that you think the other person may enjoy (but refrain from talking about how much your holiday cost you, unless the other party brings it up.)
7. Hometowns
8. About the occupation
9. Current trends in art or fashion

10. Gossip about famous people

Small talk can be a big challenge, but a little preparation and confidence is all you need. As a skilled small talker you will come across as a more open and friendly person, compared to someone who doesn't say much during social situations. Just don't overdo it because then people will find you annoying and too chatty. Small talk helps to break the ice. You could begin the conversation by asking polite personal or professional questions. Pay attention to their answers; these answers may lead you to ask more intense questions. This could lead to a healthy and a fruitful conversation.

Points that will lead you to a good conversation

1. The questions you ask should be relevant to you and to the other person—such as questions about their background, their family, etc. This opens up areas in his life that he may have in common with you, posing an opportunity to bond.
2. Be well-read and well-informed about a lot of topics. This helps you conduct a conversation with people from different backgrounds easily.
3. Keep the flow of the conversation casual. Avoid talking about politics or business, because then it becomes harder to find common ground that you can agree on. Topics should be light and cheerful, so that you get an opportunity to bond better with the other party.
4. Try to take control of the conversation by initiating topics. If you sense the other person is uncomfortable then you should try changing the topic.

APPROPRIATENESS

Appropriateness in conversation is basically about 'register'. A speaker has to use the right tone/lexis and grammar while speaking to enhance the effect of his words. The tone of the speaker has to be in sync with the:

- context
- audience and
- purpose

Appropriate use of language can help you communicate effectively. Incorrect tone and words can cause problems at work, as they can send a wrong message. Therefore, the speaker needs to be careful about not only the choice of words but also about his tone. Your body language and facial expressions also convey a lot along with your words. So, mould your body language according to your relationship with your audience, for instance, be formal when speaking to seniors and colleagues at your work place.

BUILDING RAPPORT

People do business with people they like, and the key to having someone like you is to build rapport with them. Fortunately, you can learn how to build rapport. People operate with four distinct ways of interaction. After studying these styles and interactions you will be able to analyse a person's personality, which will help you build a rapport with him/her.

There are four social styles

1. **Analyticals:** Such people seek perfection. They are organised, independent and may appear most uncommunicative. Analyticals are temperamental and sarcastic. They are reserved, but once the ice is broken they become dedicated and loyal.
2. **Commanders:** are natural leaders. They seek control. They are high achievers, can be bold and assertive, and are often very competitive. They also can be egocentric, headstrong, and short-tempered.
3. **Expressives:** are full of fun and are very open. They are very cheerful, and enthusiastic. They also can be loud, talkative, and undisciplined.
4. **Stabilisers:** are relationship builders. They seek peace. You'll often see them as accommodating, considerate and easy-going. Stabilisers will avoid conflict, sometimes at any cost.

ASSIGNMENT

1. What are the three kinds of speaking situations? Write a brief note on each.
2. What do you understand by the term 'public speaking'?
3. Define small talk? Discuss the context where small talk takes place?
4. What are the ways to master a small talk? Give examples.
5. Why is appropriateness of tone required?

Chapter 6

LISTENING SKILLS

Objectives

To introduce you to:

- The stages of the listening process
- Strategies of listening
- Types of listening
- How to be a good listener

INTRODUCTION

Listening is a process of receiving and understanding the spoken word. Listening provides the aural input that forms the basis of language acquisition and enables the learner to interact in spoken communication.

LISTENING SKILLS

Listening is different from hearing because when you hear something you don't decode and interpret the message as a bit of information. There are four stages in listening comprehension—sensing the message, decoding or interpreting it, evaluating and responding to it. The response can be oral or internalised. For example, if you are listening to the news or to a speech, you might not vocalise your thoughts, but you do respond to what is being said. When you listen to someone, you are able to understand what they are saying if you share a common language. Apart from sharing a common language code with your conversation partner, your interpretation of the message may be influenced by other factors such as your educational, social, cultural and professional conditioning. While decoding a message you not only understand the message but also take in extra-linguistic features such as the speaker's attitude and viewpoint about the topic. For example, if a manager or supervisor is not happy with the progress made in a particular project, then he is not likely to voice his displeasure very vehemently in an open forum, but which is likely to be indicated by his choice of words and his body language. These are cues that are picked up by a good listener and there are a number of listening strategies that can make you a good listener.

Developing listening skills is crucial for managers. One's listening skills help in processing the knowledge that is being relayed in a casual conversation, meetings, etc. It is a receptive skill which is of vital importance. Listening is a very effective way to establish a relationship. Active listening is to hear and understand the content and feeling of the speaker. By focusing on the content you can gather a lot of information which is being conveyed.

STAGES OF THE LISTENING PROCESS

- Hearing
- Concentrating on the message
- Comprehending, understanding and interpreting
- Analysing and evaluating
- Responding
- Recalling

LISTENING STRATEGIES

As we have mentioned above, listening strategies help us in understanding and recalling the aural or listening output. These strategies can be classified according to the manner in which the listener processes the output.

Top-down strategies

These are strategies that are listener-based and the listener dips into the background knowledge of the topic, the language, the kind of text and the context. If we revert to our earlier analogy of a manager /supervisor not being happy about the progress of a particular project; a person in the audience who is aware of the situation will try to interpret what is being heard, weigh it against their own judgement of the situation and try to anticipate what is coming. Some top-down strategies are:

- Listening for the main idea
- Predicting
- Drawing inferences
- Summarising

Bottom-up strategies

These are strategies that are text-based and the listener relies on the language of the message. By language we mean the grammar and semantics or meaning of the message. Some bottom-up strategies are :

- Listening for specific details
- Related words
- Recognising word-order patterns

TYPES OF LISTENING

Informative Listening

Informative listening is where you concentrate on the message being delivered. It involves memory and attentiveness. In this your aim is to gather a lot of information.

Relationship Listening

Relationship listening is when you listen to develop or sustain a relationship. Relationship listening is important not only in personal life but also in professional areas which require negotiation and sales.

Appreciative Listening

In appreciative listening the listener gets satisfaction from listening to the source. This source could be a good speaker or a musician. It could also be a person conveying some information which the listener needs.

Critical Listening

Critical listening is where the listener weighs the message and seeks to assess the truth of what is being said; and checks if it makes any sense and if it is of any use. It also includes checking facts and figures given in the message. Evaluative listening is particularly pertinent when the other person is trying to persuade us to do something.

Discriminative Listening

Discriminative listening is the most basic type of listening, whereby the difference between different sounds is identified. Discriminative listening is the ability to understand the subtleties of emotional variation in another person's voice. Listening is a visual as well as auditory activity, which also involves body movements and actions. Therefore, one needs to understand the body language of the person whom one is speaking too.

Comprehensive listening

By comprehensive listening we mean to understand what is being said by the speaker. Comprehensive listening is also known as content listening, informative listening and full listening.

Biased listening

Biased listening happens when the person hears only what they want to hear, typically misinterpreting what the other person says based on the stereotypes and other biases that they have. Such biased listening is often very evaluative in nature.

TO BE A GOOD LISTENER

- Do not interrupt the speaker.
- Do not divert the speaker by asking too many questions.
- Let the speaker finish and then only ask questions.
- Focus on what is being said.
- Do not be distracted by activities happening around you.

Barriers to effective listening

Effective listening is not an easy task and there are numerous obstructions or barriers to listening that a good listener should avoid.

Listeners

- Listeners who know the answer
- Listeners who know too little
- Trying to be helpful

Strategies to overcome this barrier

Listen carefully to what is being said and even if you think you know the answer, try to keep an open mind while listening and try to acquire new ideas and insights, rather than trying to stick to your own viewpoints. Don't feel out of tune if the content is intellectually or emotionally unfamiliar. Try and get the gist of the message and try and develop a positive attitude towards it. Don't try to be a problem-solver trying to help the speaker with their thoughts. Trying to help means that you have already made some value judgements about the speaker. If you think you have some genuine advice to offer, wait for the speaker to ask for it or politely seek permission after she has finished speaking.

Speakers

- Speaker's manner of delivery
- Speaker's organisation of thought
- Attitude towards the listener

Strategies to overcome this barrier

A great part of listening revolves around the way the talks or delivers his speech. Bad enunciation and disorganised thoughts often prove to be great barriers in listening there can be a breakdown in communication. In such instances try and concentrate on the subject matter rather than the mannerisms of the speaker. Speakers have different ways of organising their thoughts while explaining complex situations. Some tend to accentuate how things are different, while others tend to look at how things are alike. If speaker and hearer are on different sides of the spectrum, these differing mental attitudes can result in a breakdown of communication. An approach to overcome this barrier is to ask yourself questions on which points you agree or disagree with the speaker rather than trying to contradict the speaker's point of view.

Language

- Ambiguity
- Misinterpretation
- Red flag words

Strategies to overcome these barriers

Language never was intended to carry the same meaning to everyone and different people attach different meaning to words and this can form a barrier between speaker and hearer, howsoever unintended, leading not only to ambiguity but also misinterpretation. Certain words or 'red flag words' often trigger an unexpectedly strong association in the listener's mind, mostly because of her personal beliefs or prior life experiences. To overcome this barrier try and listen carefully to what the speaker is saying and try to see if there is any sub-text in the message. If you still feel that there is a misinterpretation and you are provoked into an emotional reaction, stop the conversation politely and clarify the point with the speaker. If it is a speech or talk, take down notes and seek a clarification later. Good listeners have learned how to minimise the distraction caused by red flag words, as often that is not the intended meaning as understood by the listener.

Distractions

Other distractions are mostly physical, such as bad acoustics, a faulty PA system or external disturbances which can be easily eliminated.

ASSIGNMENT

1. What are the different ways of listening?
2. What is critical listening?
3. Explain the stages of listening.
4. Briefly describe the barriers to effective listening.

PART III

WRITTEN COMMUNICATION

Chapter 7

LETTER WRITING

Objectives

To introduce you to:

- The importance of letter writing
- Ways of writing letters
- Kinds of business/formal letters

Business letters are an important part of professional communication. A good business letter provides pertinent information in a clear and concise manner.

This can only happen if there is clarity of thought. Therefore, one needs to ask the following questions before writing a letter:

- Why am I writing this letter?
- What is the best way to achieve this?
- What information do I need to provide? For example, dates of previous letters, date on which you saw the advertisement, dates of appointments, addresses of shops and people, names of people involved, reference or account numbers.
- What arguments do I need to use?

Business letters have a set format. The format makes it easy for the reader to comprehend the letter. It starts with a formal salutation, which is followed by the body text. Let us discuss the parts of a letter in greater detail. It is important to put the subject line after the formal greeting. The subject line should introduce the subject matter in a clear fashion.

BODY OF THE MESSAGE

A letter usually has more than one paragraph depending on the need of the communicator. The message should have a logical flow and bullet points can be given wherever relevant.

Each paragraph should focus on a separate aspect of the subject and there should be clear links between paragraphs.

The First Paragraph

The first paragraph of the letter should introduce the subject and should state the purpose of writing.

The Final Paragraph

The final paragraph should leave the reader in no doubt about the writer's take on the subject of the letter. It should be positive and unambiguous.

Achieve The Right Tone

It is very important for a business letter to have a suitable tone. It should neither be too casual nor too formal. So, as far as possible:

- Avoid jargon.
- Use shorter sentences rather than longer ones.
- Avoid using the passive. For example write, 'We sent you that letter by mistake,' rather than the more pompous, 'Our letter was sent in error.'
- Be clear and to the point, but don't be too blunt.

Adopt A Clear Layout

Adopt a letter layout that is clear and consistent. For example, if you put a comma after the person's name in the greeting, include one after 'Yours faithfully/Yours sincerely'; either indent the paragraphs or leave a space between them, without indentation.

PURPOSE OF A BUSINESS LETTER

A business letter is a formal way of communicating between two or more parties. There are many different uses and business letters. Business letters can be informational, persuasive, motivational, or promotional. Business letters should be typed and printed out on standard 8.5" x 11" white paper.

ELEMENTS OF A GOOD LETTER

The most important element of writing a good letter is to keep it simple and jargon-free. For instance if you are addressing your letter to the department of human resources, avoid using highly technical terms that only engineers would understand, even if your letter is addressed to an engineering company, chances are that the personnel in human resources does not have an engineering background.

The next element is that you make sure your present objective in a clear and concise manner. Don't be vague about your objective, most people will not have the patience to sit there and guess at the meaning of your letter or the time to read a long-winded letter, just get to the point without going into unnecessary details.

Another important element to remember is to remain professional. Even if you are writing a complaint letter, remain polite and courteous, simply state the problem(s) along with any other relevant information.

LETTER FORMAT

Your Address
Date (Month Day, Year)

Mr/Mrs/Ms/Dr Full name of recipient.
Title/Position of Recipient.
Company Name
Address

Dear Ms/Mrs/Mr Last Name

Subject: Title of Subject

First Paragraph ....
....

Second Paragraph ....
....

Final Paragraph ....
....

Closing (Sincerely...)

Signature

Your Name
Your Title

Enclosures
Typist's initials
The block format is the simplest format; all of the writing is flush against the left margin.

COMPONENTS OF A BUSINESS LETTER

1. Your address (not needed if the letter is printed on the company letterhead already on it) It is the address of the sender of the letter so the recipient can easily find out where to send a reply.
2. Date: Put the date on which the letter was written in the format 'Month Day Year', i.e., August 30, 2003.
3. Inside Address: The address of the person you are writing to along with the name of the recipient, their title and company name, if you are not sure who the letter should be addressed to either leave it blank, but try to put in a title, i.e. 'Director of Human Resources'.
4. Salutation: Dear Ms/Mrs/Mr Last Name or To Whom It May Concern (if the recipient's name is not known). Put a colon after the salutation.
5. Subject Line (optional): Leave a line space before the subject. Subject makes it easier for the recipient to find out what the letter is about.
6. Body text: The content of the letter should be systematically presented. The information should be provided in a clear and a concise manner.
7. Closing: A letter usually ends with 'Sincerely', 'Sincerely yours', 'Thank you', etc.
8. Signature: Your signature will go in this section, usually signed in black or blue ink.
9. Printed Name: Below the sender's signature, sender's name needs to be mentioned, if desired one can put one's title or position underneath it.
10. Enclosure: If the letter contains any document other than the letter itself the letter will include the word 'enclosure'. If there is more than one document that needs to be sent that the number of documents would have to be mentioned in brackets along with the word 'enclosure'.
11. Reference Initials: If a typist has typed your letter then at the end you should mention your initials in capital letters followed by the typist's initials in lower case., e.g., AG/gs or AG:gs.

SAMPLE LETTERS

519 Front Street
JVPD,
Mumbai 400053

October 5, 2004

Ms Nisha Oberoi
Accounts Payable
The Cooking Store
765 Berliner Plaza
Industrial Point
Mumbai 400078

Dear Ms Oberoi,

It has come to my notice that your company, The Cooking Store, has been making late payments for the past three months.

In order to encourage our customers to make payments before the due date, we have come up with a scheme. According to this, 2% off on the invoice amount will be provided to the customer, if the payment is done with in 10 days of receiving the invoice. I hope that everything is going well for you and your company. You are one of our biggest customers, and we esteem your association. If you have any questions, please feel free to contact me at (555) 555-555.

Yours sincerely,

Signature

Bobby Singh
Accounts Receivable

REQUESTING A LETTER OF RECOMMENDATION

Sample Letter of Recommendation

562 Banquet Street
Fair Valley, AL 81356
September 28, 2004

To Whom It May Concern

It is with great pleasure that I am recommending Rose Fernandes to you. I am the Head Sales Manager at Vacuums Plus and Rose has been under my supervision from November 2000 to August, 2004 as a salesperson.

Rose would be a great asset to any company. She is one of the brightest employees that I have ever had. She also has a great drive and passion for her work.

Rose is such a quick learner. Within her first two weeks at Vacuums Plus she had learned all the product names, their features, and how they work. It normally takes a new employee at least two months to get familiar with all the products that we sell.

Rose's drive has led her to great success at Vacuums Plus. She has had the honour of receiving the 'Top Sales Person of the Month Award' ten times in her last year at Vacuums Plus, which is a feat that no employee has ever achieved here before.

I believe that Rose Fernandes will be an excellent fit for your company. Rose has been nothing short of an exemplary employee. If you have any further questions, feel free to contact me at (555) 555-555 and I'll be happy to answer any questions you have.

Yours sincerely,

Signature

Manish Mehta
Head Sales Manager

LETTER WRITING TIPS

- Always proofread your letter after writing it, check for sentence structure, grammar, spelling mistakes, etc.

- Keep the recipient in mind, and write in a way that he/she can easily understand the letter.
- Don't use abbreviated dates, i.e., use November 19, 2004, and not 11/19/04
- Be respectful when you write, even if you are writing a letter of complaint.
- Be concise and keep to the point, but don't leave out any important information.
- Try to keep your letter short enough so that it fits on one page.
- If your letter is more than a page long, use another page, don't use the back of the page.
- If you have access to company (or personal) stationary with a letterhead on it, use that instead of regular paper.

ASSIGNMENT

1. Briefly describe the kinds of reports you have read about in this chapter.
2. Discuss the layout of a business letter.
3. Discuss the importance of a well-written business letter.
4. You are the Manager (Operations) of Oriental Pvt Ltd . Write a letter to the HR Manager of your company stating general grievances of the staff of your department.

Chapter 8

REPORT WRITING

Objectives

To introduce you to

- Kinds of reports
- Writing a report
- Sections of a report
- Summer project/internship reports

INTRODUCTION

Reports form an integral part of any profession and one is required to write different types of report as part of their profession. Virtually every job requires report writing—annual reports, monthly sales reports or production and project reports. This chapter will provide them with a basic understanding of the content and structure of reports.

KINDS OF REPORTS

A report is an essential official document that is written to investigate, present and analyse information thoroughly and logically. It is a very important part of the engineering and business disciplines; and even sciences and social sciences. Therefore, it needs to be unambiguous, accurate and organised. A report is a formatted and organised presentation of data. It usually helps in making decisions and hence is a very crucial document. It furnishes all the information that is required to make a certain decision and is prepared after doing extensive research. The objectives of a report is usually to collect information about a certain product or situation or to analyse it. Therefore reports are basically of two kinds—*information* reports and *research* reports. Lets us look at the two examples.

Information Reports: Let us assume that the productivity of a fast-selling and popular car has gone down and the general manager of the automobile company wants a report from his production manager as to why this has happened as it is affecting the company's image and giving competitors an edge. The production manager in turn asks this subordinate to prepare a report on this. The report that has to be submitted will be an information gathering report as it will contain information about this productivity say over the last three years, the present situation, look at the process of production. The purpose of the report will be to give the available data as clearly concisely and correctly as possible.

Research Reports: If we are to carry the above analogy further, we might arrive at a possible scenario. Once the production manager gets all the information in the information report, he converts it into a research report as the general manager is likely to want a solution to the problem. His task will be to analyse available data, and then make recommendations in order to solve the problem. He might for example find that the number of people working on the assembly line has gone down in the past years due to cost cutting measures or that a particular vendor is delaying in sending a component that is needed in the manufacturing process. The purpose of a research report is to enable the writer to suggest/take action on the basis of the new information presented in the report.

One needs to be clear on the following points before preparing a report:

- Purpose of the report.
- Who will be reading the report?
- Proper research needs to be done.
- The problem/subject that needs to be discussed in the report should be closely analysed and suitable recommendations should be made.

WRITING A REPORT

Report writing is a time-consuming but an important job. Before writing, organise the information that needs to be put in the report. Sort out the gathered information and begin writing. Write a rough draft first and then re-work on it till you are satisfied.

Remember that you have to:

- Define the project or problem.
- Give the background.
- Provide adequate supporting data.
- State your recommendations.

ATTRIBUTES OF A GOOD REPORT

Clear: Your report should be easy to follow. Keep the format and even language simple. The thought process should also be lucidly given and easy to understand. If the readers of your report are not experts, then avoid using technical terms.

Accurate: Accuracy in a report not only includes accuracy of data provided but also accuracy of writing. As reports are used to make decisions, inaccurate data can lead to inaccurate decisions. Therefore, be very sure about the source, while collecting data. Also present in a manner that is easy to comprehend.

Easy-to-access: Your report should be well–organised and all the information should be presented in such a fashion that it is easy-to-access. Use appropriate headings, annexure, graphs and tables, etc. Make sure that there is a table of contents at the beginning as it really saves time while locating a certain topic in the report. All these will help the reader access the required information easily.

SECTIONS OF A REPORT

Title. At the beginning of a report, its title needs to be mentioned. The title is usually the subject or problem that the report is on. It should not carry a very oblique title that makes it incomprehensible and not in line with the content of the report.

Summary. Give a clear and a very concise account of the main points, conclusions and recommendations. It should be short and to-the-point. It helps senior managers who do not have the time to go through the entire report to get a gist of what the report is talking about. It should be free from jargon and brief.

Introduction. In this section you need to give the background to 'the problem' and you need to show the reader why the report is important to them. Explain to them how the details that follow are arranged.

Main Body. This section presents the process of deriving logical conclusions to your problem. It will probably have several sections and even sub-sections with clearly indicated headers and titles. These sections again, should be organised in a coherent and logical fashion. The information should be arranged logically, and the data should be presented in order of priority. This section is most likely to be read by experts so you can use technical terms and jargon, but it is always better to explain what it means before you use it. You may choose to include a 'discussion', in which you can explain the significance of your findings.

Conclusion. In this section, present the inferences of your investigation. Use simple language to discuss your conclusions.

Recommendations. In this section you offer solutions to the problem being discussed.State your recommendations in order of priority, and in simple language.

Appendices. Put the heavy details here, the information that only specialists will see. As a guide, if some detail is essential to your argument then include it in the main body, if it merely supports the argument then it could go in an appendix.

Conclusions and Recommendations

In the conclusion, remember that readers expect certain information to be in certain places. They do not expect them to hunt for what they want and the harder one makes it for them the more likely they are to toss the report to one side and ignore it. So what should we do?

1. Follow the generally accepted format for a report: Summary, Introduction, Main Body, Conclusions, Recommendations and Appendices.
2. Organise your information in each section in a logical fashion with the reader in mind, usually putting things in order of priority—most important first.

WRITING A SUMMER PROJECT/INTERNSHIP REPORT

Every management academy has a different way / representation of summer internship reports. This section provides a standard report structure with reference to MBA in Marketing field. This will give you a brief idea of how a summer internship report for MBA grades is structured.

1. Cover and Title page
   - Certificate
   - Acknowledgement
   - Declaration given by the student
   - Table of contents
   - Executive summary
2. Introduction to the project
   - Introduction
   - Objective of the study
   - Methodology
   - Chapter contents
   - Sources of data
   - Sample size, if any
   - Methods of data collection
   - Instrument used
   - Tools and techniques of analysis
3. Literature review

   In this section you will have to mention the ways in which organisational realities are similar or different from theory. The management theory dealt with in the report must be written in detail.

   - The Background
   - The Promoters
   - The Company and its Product line

- Features of the Product
- Marketing strategies
- Competitors
- Government Policies
- Taxation aspects
- Major problems
- Achievements
- Share Market position
- National and International Image
- Future Prospects
- Conclusion

4. About the project (assignment or topic) taken in the organisation
5. Surveys, Feedback and Data Analysis
6. Suggestion/ Recommendation
7. Conclusion
8. Bibliography
9. Appendix/Annexure

If you have used tables, graphs, or/and figures, then you have to provide the information of the source from which it has been taken.

The report is actually the most important part of summers. No matter how much hard work you have put in, if the report is not done well, all your efforts are wasted.

Therefore, take at least 7-10 days of your training period for planning and preparing the report. Check out the standard formats for report writing.

Make sure that the language of your report is simple; and that it is organised in a logical fashion and covers the entire scope of the project.

Whatever you have learnt from and during your summer training should reflect in your report. Different theories could be used to have a sound analysis and they should be mentioned in the report.

Every individual has a different way of presenting a report. You have to make sure that your report reflects theoretical implementation of marketing principles. Don't worry even if you are placed for a summer project where you are not able to contribute much with your theoretical knowledge. Remember its better to make initiatives and work forward so that your report reflects some thing that is more relevant.

Remember, numbers speak more than the theoretical lines. Try to show what effect your recommendations can make in the organisation in terms of numbers.

For instance:

'After the analysis of call centre activities of my company, I realised that lot of time was wasted. My recommendations will reduce this wastage by 31%.'

A report of this kind should be more graphical. Rather than writing down observations in the form of points, try to make use of graphs. This will depict the results at a glance and have better impact.

FINAL TIPS

- Plan extensively for summer training in terms of choosing the right organisation and right project.
- Take summer training seriously. It's your first brush with corporate life.
- Use the opportunity to network with experts in the field of study.
- Try and understand the organisation set-up, broad strategy, culture, etc. This will help you in final placements. Prepare a detailed note on the organization.
- Keep in touch with your mentor/guide.
- Do not hesitate to ask in case you don't know something, because you are not expected to know everything anyway.
- A quality project done could be your passport to final placement.
- Report writing is as critical as doing the project; therefore, plan for at least 7–10 days for giving your report a shape.
- If your project has relevance to people outside your campus and the organisation, that you could share the synopsis, provided it is allowed by your organisation.
- Prepare a comprehensive list of vital information on the organisation that you worked for during the summer training. This will be important for job interviews. Do not leave this for the last day before the placement week.

ASSIGNMENT

1. Why are reports important in professional studies?
2. What is a business report and how do they contribute to the growth of the student?
3. What precautions are to be considered while writing a report?
4. Summer Internship Reports play very important role in final placements, illustrate.

Chapter 9

NOTICES AND CIRCULARS

Objectives

To introduce you to:

- Kinds of notices and circulars
- The importance of notices and circulars
- Ways of writing notices and circulars

INTRODUCTION

Although meetings are a prominent feature of the corporate world, managers are usually skeptical about their usefulness. However, a meeting can be productive and can be the best way to resolve issues, if conducted properly. A meeting should have a clear purpose and an agenda. Chosen participants should be formally invited by issuing a notice.

According to the Companies Act such notices, should specify the day, date, time and the venue of the meeting, and should be sent to the participants a week before the meeting is to be held. Notices draw attention to some event that will take place at some time in the future. The required information should be mentioned in a concise and an accurate manner.

WHAT IS A NOTICE?

It is usually an announcement of an event. It includes necessary information about the event keeping in mind the requirements of the management as well as the employees.

A notice should mention the name and address of the organisation, and the date on which it is issued, besides indicating the day, date, time and venue of the meeting. The business to be transacted should be mentioned in the notice, if the number of items is small then it should be indicated on the same sheet; otherwise it should be indicated on a separate sheet and enclosed with the notice as an annexure.

The notice for a meeting must specify the following:

a. Date, time and place of the meeting;
b. name of the company;
c. type of meeting;
d. authority by which notice is issued;
e. name and signature of the person issuing the notice;
f. matters to be discussed at the meeting;
g. in the case of special business, an explanatory statement;
h. purpose and agenda;
i. date of issue of the notice;
j. any enclosures required to be sent with the notice.

BENEFITS OF A NOTICE

1. Notices and circulars inform the members about the subject of the meeting in advance. This helps participants to prepare for it.
2. A notice can also be circulated to inform the employees of an organisation, about an important information or events. This keeps them aware about the happenings in the company.
3. It is precise and therefore, ensures that only matters relevant to the topic are informed.
4. It ensures that every point is properly taken up for discussion.
5. It ensures that the meeting is organised in a cordial, formal and a clear manner.

A proper notice for a meeting must be sent to every person entitled to attend and vote at the meeting. A meeting is not properly convened unless a notice of the meeting is sent well in advance. It should have a formal tone and should be simple, brief and clear.

FORMAT OF A NOTICE

NOTICE

NAME OF THE INSTITUTION

Date
Place

Information that needs to be conveyed

Sign
(name)
Designation

TYPES OF NOTICES

Notice for a Board Meeting

Notice for a meeting of the Board of Directors must be given in writing to each director at his/her address. It is prepared by the company secretary in consultation with the chairperson.

Example:

NOTICE
ABC LIMITED
21,Bikhaji Cama Place
New Delhi 110056

27 April 2007
Delhi

A meeting of the Board of Directors of the company will be held on May 10, 2007 at 4 pm at the registered office of the company in the conference room. We will consider, approve and take on record the unaudited quarterly financial results of the company. Kindly make it convenient to attend.

B.K. Shayam
(B.K. Shayam)
Company Secretary

Notice for Annual General Meeting

A notice for the annual general body meeting is given at least two weeks before the meeting is held. The notice must include the date, time and place of the meeting. It must specify whether the participant is entitled to attend and vote at the meeting. Copies of annual accounts, Directors' report and auditors' report are sent along with the notice.

Example:

NOTICE
XYZ LIMITED
NEW DELHI

August 10, 2009
Delhi

Notice is hereby given that the twenty-first annual general meeting of the company will be held on September 11, 2009 at 11 am at Air Force Auditorium, Subroto Park, New Delhi. Copy of the agenda is attached herewith.

B.P. Sharma

B.P. Sharma
Company Secretary

Notes:

1. Transfer books and register of members will be closed from August 12,2009 to September 11,2009.
2. Dividend when declared and sanctioned for payment will be payable on August 12, 2009.

Notices for General Staff

Notices for general staff are generally pinned up on a wall/notice-board. This is a popular and an effective way of reaching out to the office employees. Some notices put forward proposals, policy decisions, etc. and therefore might require staffs' signature, depicting their support and acceptance.

Example:

NOTICE
MODERN FOOD INDUSTRIES
Lawrence Road, New Delhi

15 October 2009
Delhi

All the members of staff are cordially invited to attend the farewell of Mr Sinha on October 25, 09, Friday at 7:00 pm in the main hall. Please sign to confirm that you will be attending it.

A.K. Madan
A.K. MADAN
Secretary

A notice should have a tone of request rather than of command. It should be polite and persuasive, especially if they wish the staff to confirm certain arrangements.

Example:

'Members of staff are requested to...'

'All workers are cordially invited...'

Notices Seeking Opinion

A copy of an opinion-seeking notice is usually given to each staff member; so that they can fill it and give their comments on the specified matter. For this purpose the secretary has to prepare a notice stating the available options and requesting the employees for their opinions, comments and suggestions. For example, an organisation decides to celebrate fifteenth anniversary of the company and the management wants to celebrate the occasion by involving the staff. They decide to give the following options to their employees:

1. Grand evening dinner
2. Day coach trip(staff only)
3. An evening party for staff members and their families

The secretary then, will have to draft a notice which, draws the staffs' attention to the event. He needs to mention clearly the various options provided by the management and also gives an opportunity to the employees to indicate their preference and further give suggestions.

NOTICE
HIMALAYA DRUG COMPANY
SHIMLA
STAFF CIRCULAR

15 July 2009
Shimla

It is our company's anniversary on August 12, 2009. We would like to know how you wish to celebrate the same. Some suggestions have been mentioned below. Please either mark your preference or provide a suggestion.

- Day trip by coach to scenic spot/place of interest (staff only)
- Grand evening dinner
- An evening party for staff members and their families

Please sign and return this circular by July 31

Thank you

Shyam Lal

Secretary

A notice or a circular is a formal document that informs the employees about a new activity, event or a happening. It helps the management to reach out to the members of their organisation. It is a fast and effective way of reaching out to members of an organisation as, unlike a letter, it is addressed to a large number of people. It also helps in getting employees' suggestions that would indeed prove to be beneficial and facilitate the growth of the organisation.

ASSIGNMENT

1. List the benefits of a notice for a meeting?
2. What are the important contents of a notice?
3. Draft a notice to inform the employees about a meeting, to discuss the company's performance.
4. Draft a circular requesting the employees to observe punctuality so as to increase overall efficiency of the company.

Chapter 10

RESUME WRITING

Objectives

To introduce you to:

- The basic idea of a resume
- The benefits of a well-written resume
- The parts of a resume

INTRODUCTION

A resume introduces you to a potential employer. It is a document that contains a summary of your education and work experience. It is typically used by an employer to screen applicants. Therefore, it has to be precise and clear. It should present your skills and work experience in such a fashion that an employer can see, at a glance, how you will contribute to the employer's workplace, if hired.

An effective resume is clearly focused on a specific job title and addresses the employer's stated requirements for the position. It is well-organised and to the point.

A resume is often the first line of contact. Thus it is an important document which establishes a first impression of a potential job candidate on the hirer. If written well, it may convince the reader that the candidate is ideally suited for the job. When coupled with an effective cover letter, the resume can be a very strong marketing tool.

PREPARING A RESUME

Your resume might not get you the job but it can certainly secure your chances of being seen and interviewed. Always treat it as a marketing tool. It should accurately convey your hiring value (for the specific position).

Keep the following points in your mind before preparing your resume:

- It should not be difficult to follow.
- It should be precise and not very lengthy
- It should be well-organised so that it captures the employer's interest.

Skills

While preparing your resume keep in mind the post you are applying for. You should understand the needs of the position, and if you recognise the company's need.

As in any type of marketing material, it is important to present the information so that it captures your employer's interest quickly. Your goal is to encourage the reader to stay with your document as long as possible. One of the best ways to accomplish this is to create a Summary Section at the beginning of your resume. This section will tell the reader about those personal and professional skills you possess and will highlight those skills that allow you to excel in the post applied for. Skills should be listed in such a fashion that they set you apart from your competing candidates, particularly candidates with similar skills.

Employer

When writing your resume, keep in mind your specific reader, i.e., the employer/company. Listing information that will be of no value to the position or company being targetted is just a waste of time and space.

Your potential employer is most interested in seeing how hiring you will benefit him/her and the company. Your resume should make them feel that you are the right person for the job. They should, while screening your resume, feel that they are making the right choice. Employers these days do not want to waste revenue on hiring and training people. So they are very particular about who they are employing or rather even calling for an interview.

The most effective way to do this is by identifying how you have benefited employers in the past and listing them cleverly in your resume. Let the reader know about your participation and accomplishments.

Presentation

The layout of your resume is extremely important. Your resume needs to maintain a clean and professional appearance. It should allow the reader to access the information with ease and quickly. Ensure that there are neat margins, adequate space between sections and subsections, and indenting to highlight text. Be careful while using 'bolding' and 'italics'. Overuse of these features often diminishes their effectiveness.

Put your complete contact information as it is the most important element in the document. Make sure your name, address, phone number, and e-mail address are clearly visible. It should be ideally mentioned at the top of the document. It is beneficial to add your name and phone number on additional pages as there are always chances of these sheets to become separated and get lost.

Length

The standards for resume length have changed. Earlier resumes were to be one-page in length and not longer. But this would make the resume of the candidates with years of experience look messy and unreadable. These days this one-page rule no longer exists.

Now, one can use as much space as you need to concisely, accurately, and effectively communicate one's education, skills, employment history, achievements, and other accomplishments. The length of a resume doesn't make a difference anymore till the time the information furnished is relevant and valuable to the employer.

Mention in detail, your most recent employment and accomplishments. Always talk about your growth in a company where multiple positions have been held. Cite promotions and increased responsibilities. List positions held prior to this but there isn't a need to provide their details. This section is usually referred as 'Work Experience' and is the most valuable part of resume. It has to power to entice the reader call you for an interview. If this section is not impressive enough then you might loose a good opportunity or a position.

Once called for an interview, you will have an opportunity to expand on the information mentioned in your resume.

RESUME FORMAT

Given below is the most frequently used format

CONTACT INFORMATION

Name

Address

Phone, Fax

E-mail id

OBJECTIVE

This should be short and crisp. It is a statement of your goals for employment, and it typically forms the first section of a resume. Stating an objective is optional. However, it helps to convince your potential employer that you know what you want and are familiar with the field. It can also mention the kind of employment you are looking for.

WORK EXPERIENCE

List your work experience here.

EDUCATIONAL QUALIFICATIONS

Qualifications need to be mentioned here

EXTRACURRICULAR ACTIVITIES

Mention your extracurricular activities so that the reader knows what all you are good at and how actively you participate in other activities and programmes. It just gives them an impression about how enthusiastic you are.

HOBBIES

Informs the reader about the kind of person you are.

REFERENCES

If required

DATE AND SIGNATURE

Given below is a sample resume of an HR employee:

Rati Singh

House no:112, RM Road, Pitam Pura, Delhi

Tel no.: 91-999933333 (M), 011-3294410 (R)

Email: rsingh32@gmail.com

OBJECTIVE

To continuously enhance my knowledge base and be an active contributing member in an organisation that provides me challenging work and growth opportunities.

ACADEMIC CREDENTIALS

- PGDBM (Post Graduate Diploma in Business Management) from MNA, Delhi (2004-2005)
- MA in Economics from ABC University (2002–2004)
- B. Com (Hons) from X College, University (1999–2002)

WORK EXPERIENCE

I. XYZ Consultants Pvt. Ltd.

Designation: Team Member

Period: November 2006-till date

Job Responsibilities

- Screening and scrutinising candidates, profiles on the basis of their expertise.
- Updating and maintaining the database of XYZ for the given specialised vertical-HR.
- Sourcing candidates from References and Head Hunting.
- Conducting preliminary interviews, and responsible for short-listing suitable candidates.
- Short-listing of resumes as per client requirement from current database.
- Delivering HR Mandates demanded by our clients efficiently and on time.
- Exhaustive Resume mining on Job Portals like Monster India, Naukri, Times Jobs.
- Evaluating and generating reports and providing detailed information of clients' mandate handled by me.
- Conducting telephonic interviews of prospective candidates.
- Preparing MIS Reports.

II. S. N. Sons and Co.

Designation: Senior Executive Assistant

Period: May 2003-October 2006

Job Responsibilities

- Co-ordinating Recruitment Process in the organisation
- Handling all pre-joining and joining formalities followed by Induction Programme at all levels.
- Conducting reference checks.
- Maintaining leave records and absenteeism data of employees.
- Verifying title documents of customers of our clients (like Citibank, SBI etc.) from a legal perspective and preparing reports thereon.
- Drafting of Mortgage Deeds.
- Preparing presentation for clients.
- Coordinating Training Sessions.
- One point contact for clients regarding service quality and general queries.

SKILLS

- Good Public Relation skills
- Quality team player
- Strong analytical abilities
- Well polished business etiquettes

ACHIEVEMENTS AND ACTIVITIES

- Scored highest marks in HR project in PGDBM.
- Topped in Economics in final year of graduation.
- Pursued positive attitude and public speaking course from 'Positive thinking'.
- Executive Member of Dramatics Society in College (1999–2000).

PERSONAL INFORMATION

Date of Birth:	August 10, 1982
Languages Known:	English and Hindi
Marital Status:	Single
Interests:	Making friends and listening to music

Date Rati Singh

COVERING LETTER

A cover letter is a letter that you send along with your CV when you apply for a job. An impressive covering letter along with a good resume might improve your chances of selection.

The cover letter is the first thing that the recruiter reads when short-listing resumes. It is much shorter than a resume and, if well-written could grab the attention of the person reading it. Your cover letter should highlight the value you offer to meet the employer needs. In a covering letter, briefly introduce yourself, state what position you are applying for and where you saw it advertised. You could also specify the type of work you are looking for; explain why you're interested in this type of work, demonstrating an understanding of what it's likely to involve. Highlight the ways in which you are suitable for this position. Take the opportunity, if necessary, to explain any anomalies in your background, such as any time gaps or any other ways in which you don't match the selection criteria.

Here is a sample covering letter for you.

Dear Madam,

I have recently shifted to Mumbai and am looking for a job. I have four years of experience in mainstream publishing of which last two years has been with Write & Co Pvt Ltd. I have a masters in English Literature from ABC University.

Please find attached my resume. Kindly let me know if you have an appropriate position for me. I would love to be a part of your organisation.

I look forward to hearing from you.

Thank you

With regards
Roshini Mehta

ASSIGNMENT

1. What is a resume? What do you think your resume should reflect?
2. What are the important contents of a resume?
3. A resume has to be to the point and easy to follow. Discuss.
4. Draft a resume of a sales executive seeking an employment as Senior Sales Executive in ABCL Ltd
5. You are a marketing executive seeking a position of marketing manager in pharmaceutical company. Draft a covering letter highlighting your skills.

Chapter 11

PARAGRAPH WRITING

Objectives

To enable you to

- Express your thoughts clearly
- Put down your thoughts point wise
- Write effectively

INTRODUCTION

In general, the purpose of a paragraph is to express one point, idea or opinion.

This main idea is expressed through three sections of a paragraph:

1. *Beginning or the introduction topic sentence:* Here the writer discusses his idea and introduces the main subject of consideration.
2. *Middle supporting details:* In the section the idea is explained and discussed in detail.
3. *End closing sentence:* Make your point again.

PURPOSE

The purpose of any paragraph is to express an idea. Most paragraphs consist of a few related sentences.

Planning a Paragraph

You can write a successful paragraph by starting off with a plan. The key to composing a successful paragraph is to break it down into short, simple steps.

- Subject of your paragraph
  Write down the subject of your paragraph. To express your subject, write only a word or phrase.
- Pre-writing for your paragraph
  Begin by brainstorming. Brainstorming doesn't involve writing complete sentences or paragraphs. Brainstorming involves coming up with ideas using words or short phrases.

Writing a paragraph

A paragraph should contain a single idea and the sentences should be arranged in some order. When you are pre-writing a paragraph, keep the topic in mind and what you would want to say about. This helps you to order the sentences properly, as sentences within a paragraph cannot be placed randomly.

The topic sentence

The topic introduces the idea and should also give a brief outline of the paragraph. This sentence is very crucial as it has to grab the reader's attention. Therefore, it should be drafted properly and should be well-planned. Once you have the topic sentence ready, it is easy to structure the rest of the paragraph.

First paragraph

The first paragraph of the body should include the strongest argument, most significant examples, cleverest illustration. The subject for this paragraph should be in the first or second sentence. This subject should relate to the main subject of the essay.

Second paragraph

The second paragraph of the body should include the second strongest argument, second most significant example, second cleverest illustration, or an obvious follow up the first paragraph in the body. The first sentence of this paragraph should contain the reverse hook, which ties in with the transitional hook at the end of the first paragraph of the body. The topic for this paragraph should be in the first or second sentence. This topic should relate to the thesis statement in the introductory paragraph. The last sentence in this paragraph should include a transitional hook to tie into the third paragraph of the body.

Third paragraph

The third paragraph of the body should include the weakest argument, weakest example, weakest illustration, or an obvious follow up to the second paragraph in the body. The first sentence of this paragraph should contain the reverse hook, which ties in with the transitional hook at the end of the second paragraph. The topic for this paragraph should be in the first or second sentence. This topic should relate to the thesis statement in the introductory paragraph. The last sentence in this paragraph should include a transitional concluding hook that signals the reader that this is the final major point being made in this essay. This hook also leads into the concluding paragraph.

Concluding paragraph

The fifth paragraph is the summary paragraph. It is important to restate the thesis and three supporting ideas in an original and powerful way as this is the last chance the writer has to convince the reader of the validity of the information presented.

AN EXAMPLE OF PARAGRAPH WRITING

Example

Stephen King, creator of such stories as Carrie and Pet Sematary, stated that the Edgar Allan Poe stories he read as a child gave him the inspiration and instruction he needed to become the writer that he is. Poe , as does Stephen King, fills the reader's imagination with the images that he wishes the reader to see, hear, and feel. His use of vivid, concrete visual imagery to present both static and dynamic settings and to describe people is part of his technique. Poe's short story "The Tell-Tale Heart" is a story about a young man who kills an old man who cares for him, dismembers the corpse, then goes mad when he thinks he hears the old man's heart beating beneath the floor boards under his feet as he sits and discusses the old man's absence with the police. In "The Tell-Tale Heart," a careful reader can observe Poe's skillful manipulation of the senses.

This paragraph should include the following:

1. An allusion to the pattern used in the introductory paragraph.
2. A restatement of the thesis statement, using some of the original language or language that "echoes" the original language. (The restatement, however, must not be a duplicate thesis statement.)
3. A summary of the three main points from the body of the essay.
4. A final statement that gives the reader signals that the discussion has come to an end. (This final statement may be a "call to action" in a persuasive essay.)

The **introductory paragraph** includes a paraphrase of something said by a famous person in order to get the reader's attention. The second sentence leads up to the thesis statement which is the third sentence. The thesis statement (sentence 3) presents topic of the paper to the reader and provides a mini-outline. The topic is Poe's use of visual imagery. The mini-outline tells the reader that this paper will present Poe's use of imagery in three places in his writing: (1) description of static setting; (2) description of dynamic setting; and (3) description of a person. The last sentence of the paragraph uses the words "manipulation" and "senses" as transitional hooks.

In paragraph writing we have to emphasize the idea and its coherence with the subordinate ideas. In order to have uniformity in the paragraph writing, we must ensure that we organise our thoughts in a logical way that would develop the topic of the paragraph in a more comprehensive manner.

ASSIGNMENT

1. Discuss briefly the elements of a paragraph.
2. Develop the ideas/themes into paragraphs-
3. Air pollution is a health hazard.
4. The new millennium has brought new challenges.
5. Accidents in factories result from ignorance of safety regulations.
6. Commercialising Indian sports.

Chapter 12

WRITING E-MAILS

Objectives

To enable you to:

- Understand the structure of e-mails
- Follow e-mail etiquette
- Become proficient in writing e-mails

INTRODUCTION

The emergence of business organisations with large setups has lead to the fast adoption of electronic mediums of communication. Electronic mail or e-mail as it is more commonly known is fast replacing conventional forms of letter writing or conventional postal mail both in sending personal letters as well as business communication. With the revolution in information technology (IT), more and more people are spending time on the Internet; and of all Internet activities, e-mail is the most popular. According to a survey conducted by the UCLA center for communication Policy (The UCLA Internet Report: Surveying the Digital Future, UCLA center for communication Policy, 2001) 88 per cent of all Internet users in the US, use e-mail. And according to the same survey, approximately 90 per cent of those who use the Internet at work use it to access business mail. Undoubtedly, due to its high speed, easy accessibility, low cost and efficiency, the e-mail has become one of the most important channels of communication, replacing older form of communication. It is no wonder that more and more business organisations are using the e-mail for inter and intra-office communication.

The structure of e-mails

As most of you who write e-mails know, an e-mail enables you to send a message to someone anywhere in the world without even knowing where they are located, and can expect them to receive the message almost instantaneously. Subscribers to e-mail services are called users and are recognised by their e-mail addresses which are also known as e-mail ids. You can subscribe to services like Gmail or Yahoo, or can use Outlook Express which comes as part of the MS Word package. Else you can be a part of your organisation's portal, like the one shown below.

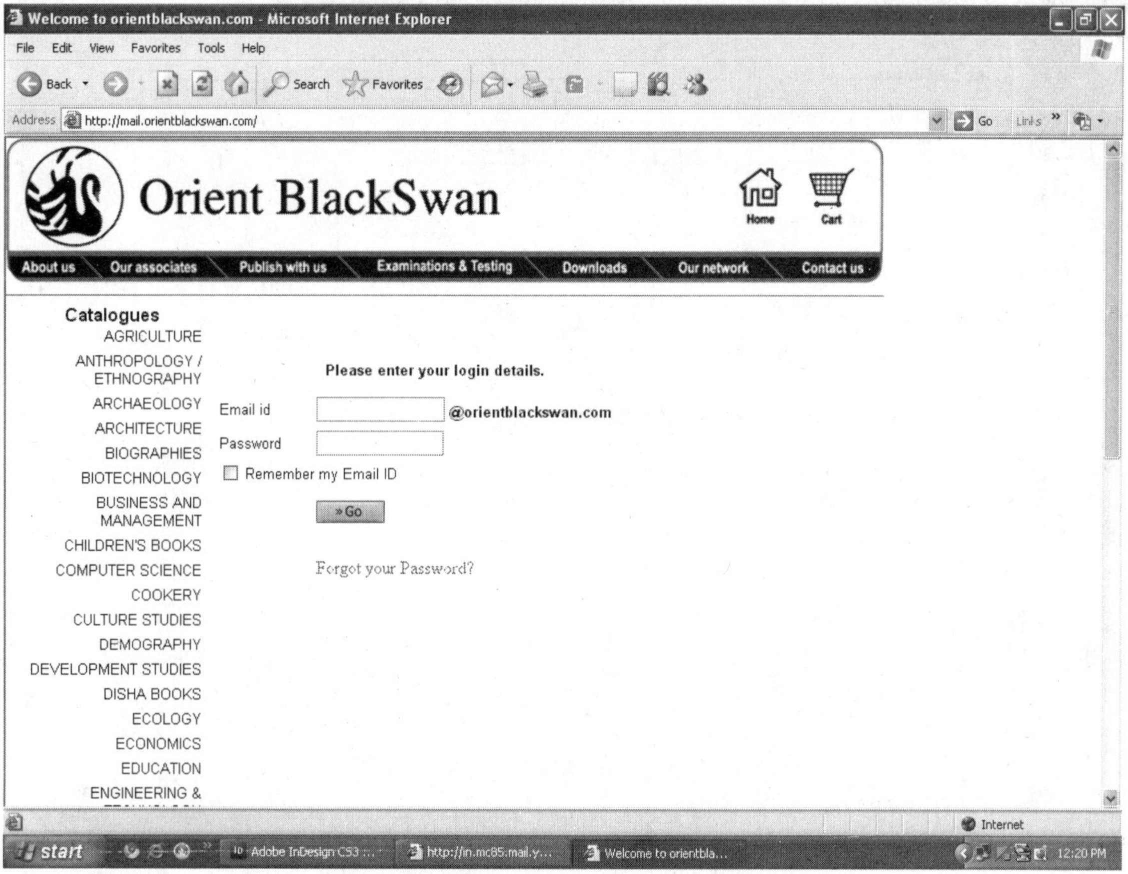

Figure 1 An e-mail portal

Several basic components make up e-mail systems, which include sender's and recipient's addresses and a subject line which explains the purpose of the message and a line indicating whether an attachment has been sent or not. In addition, there is a 'Cc' (carbon copy) line, where the address of someone to whom you want to send an additional copy is given. 'Bcc' (blind carbon copy) indicates the recipient of your message, whose name you do not want to disclose to the original and other recipients. When an e-mail is sent, the program usually inserts the sender's name, e-mail address and date, so, unlike in a conventional letter there is no need to type in this information, though in many formal correspondences, the date and place is written within the body of the message. The signature line of an e-mail message usually only has the name. However, it may sometimes contain the sender's designation and the name of the organisation which appears by default as shown in the figure below.

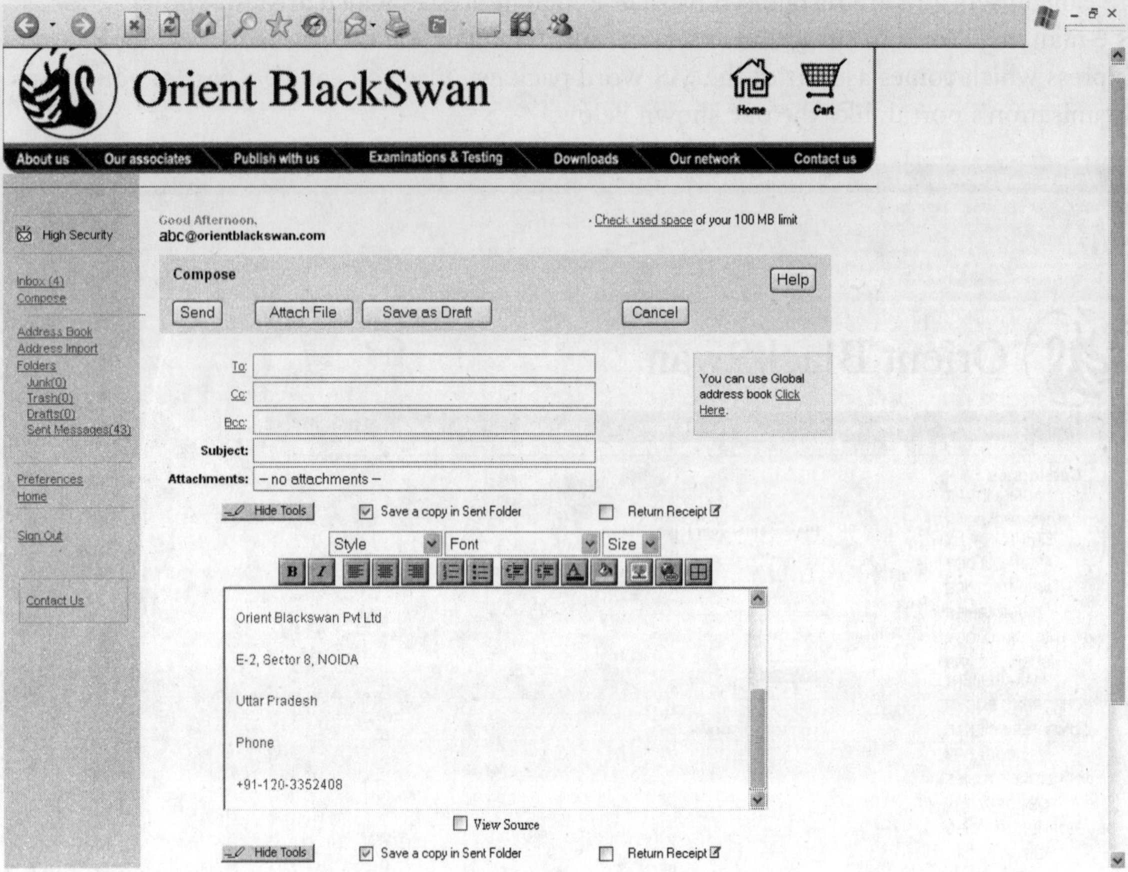

Figure 2 Components of an e-mail

Kinds of e-mail messages

E-mails, as we have mentioned earlier, are replacing conventional forms of communication, and because of the inherent advantages of speed and accessibility professionals may have to write a number of e-mails everyday. Here is a list of purposes for which e-mails are usually used:

- Announcing and advertising the arrival of a new product to business associates, clients
- Requesting information
- Sending invitations for a seminar, launch, conference or meeting
- Giving instructions on how to prepare for a meeting
- Asking for action to be taken
- Requesting/giving feedback, suggestions or recommendations

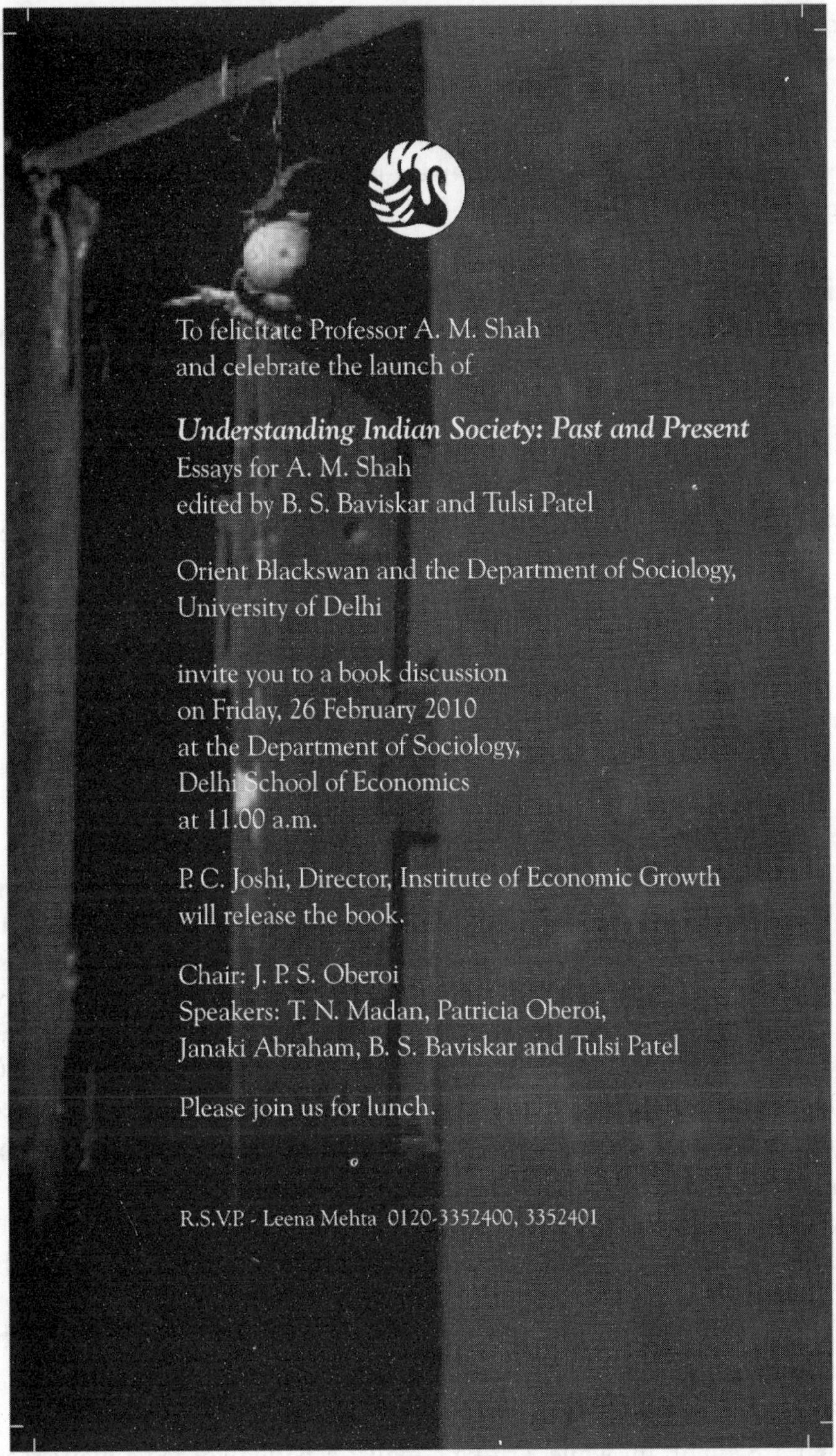

Figure 3 An invitation sent as a e-mail

Conventions of writing e-mail combine some of the characteristics of writing and speaking for as a user you have the immediacy of communicating directly with your receiver and expecting an immediate response. This perhaps explains the somewhat informal tone of an e-mail, but since e-mails are being increasingly used for business communication, care needs to be taken not to overdo it. Effective e-mail users therefore are careful about how they compose their messages.

E-mail etiquette

Guidelines are issued by most organisations to maintain certain norms regarding the transmission of electronic messages and issue guidelines to their employees. Such norms help to protect the organisation from possible liability and defamation. Disclaimers at the bottom of e-mails are written for this purpose.

An example of a disclaimer is given below.

The contents of this e-mail and any attachments may contain confidential or legally privileged information. If you are not the intended recipient, please return it to the sender immediately and do not disclose or make use of or rely on this information.

In most organisations e-mail is not used to send confidential matter like confidential employee reports, business strategies and secrets and sensitive personal business dealings, in short anything that the company does not want to disclose publicity. It is important to familiarise yourself with the established e-mail conventions of your organisation and adhere to them.

Here are some points that will help you become a professional e-mail user.

Be prompt in checking your mailbox. As e-mails are intended for speedy communication, try and check your mailbox as frequently as possible, preferably daily. Even while you are travelling, try and check your e-mails. Access to e-mails is not a problem as most important hubs have Internet facilities and if you are carrying your own laptop, you can use a data card that gives you access to the net. If you go on leave and do not want to be disturbed, it is polite that you communicate this in the form of an automated 'Out of office reply'. If the response to an e-mail is complicated or you need to consult someone else about it, send a mail saying you have received it and will respond in a day or two.

Be brief and to the point. Do not write e-mails that are too long as reading from a screen is more difficult than from the printed page. If, however, the message is such, that the mail becomes lengthy, apologise. Being brief does not mean abbreviate or write in the way you would send a text message. 'Plz send me info abt ur bks.' is not likely to create a good impression. You can be brief without being impolite. And if you are writing a business mail, avoid using emoticons, which are all right if you are writing to a friend.

Use proper spelling, punctuation and grammar. We should keep in mind that spelling and grammar are important while writing e-mails. A badly worded e-mail creates a bad impression and may be consigned to the 'trash' bin. If your program has a spell checking option, use it or look up a dictionary.

12 November 2009

The salutation is either by name to an individual or as 'Dear All'.

Dear

Annual Meeting of the Tertiary ELT, Literature, Social Sciences and Indian Languages Division: 16 – 18 December 2009

Adequate space between para-graphs.

You are requested to make it convenient to come to Hyderabad to attend the annual meeting of the **Tertiary ELT, Literature, Social Sciences and Indian Languages** division to be held **from 16 to 18 December 2009**. Please make it convenient to arrive in Hyderabad before 8 am on 16 December and to leave office (note, leave the office not Hyderabad any time after 5.30 pm) on 18 December 2009.

The Tertiary ELT, Literature, Social Sciences and Indian Languages Sales and Editorial Meeting will focus on the books published from 1 October to 15 December 2009 to date and titles approved for publication in the next three quarters. It will also closely examine our publishing and list building, on identifying the requirements of universities and ensuring that the two match. We request you to come prepared with information on gaps in the market and leads for publishing textbooks in all the fields mentioned above (ELT, Literature etc).

You are requested to collect and bring in specific information from universities in your region. Please note that incorrect information will lead to a great deal of wastage in terms of finance and time. Therefore, please ensure that you collect correct, accurate, up-to-date and valid information.

Important points are bulleted

Please ensure that you bring copies of:

- the latest syllabuses from the universities in your region
- copies of our competitors' titles which are the market leaders in your regions in each of the subjects we publish in

The outstation participants may book their to and fro train tickets immediately on receipt of this letter and confirm their arrival/departure details. The stay for all outstation participants has been arranged at:

Hotel Central Park
H. No. 3-5-863 & 864
Old M. L. A. Quarters Road
Hyderguda, Himayatnagar
Hyderabad - 500 029
Phone : +(91)-(40)-66664567
e-Mail : bdm@thehotelcentralpark.com

Lengthy note sent as attachment. Mention within the text that an attachment is being sent.

The agenda for the meeting is being sent separately.

With best wishes,

B M Mohammed Ali

Senior Vice President (SSET)

BMMA/mmr

Figure 4 An intra-office e-mail

Be careful with attachments. Do not send attachments unless they are absolutely necessary as attachments are likely to carry viruses and people wary of opening them. If the attachment is too big, try and put it in a zip file (a compressed archive). Mention within your message that you are sending an attachment, as people might miss out on it. And above all do not send an attachment (or even a message for that matter) without permission from the original sender.

Content and manner. As in conventional letter writing, be careful about the structure and layout of your message. In the case of e-mails this is all the more important, as it is more difficult reading from the screen than from the printed page. Space your paragraphs properly and if you are making points, bulletise or number them. Do not overuse the 'high priority' option or mark your mails as 'urgent' or 'important', as you might come across as aggressive. Do not write in CAPITALS, as this sounds impolite. Try and use the active voice rather than the passive; 'Your request will be looked into.' sounds more formal than 'We will look into your request at the earliest.' When replying to an e-mail, check whether all the respondents need to be copied in. Use the 'reply to all' option judiciously. Use a meaningful subject for the subject line, so that it becomes easy for the receiver to relate to it and also archive it.

Copying your e-mails to others. Be judicious about copying your e-mail to other people and do not overuse the 'cc' option. When you are copying your mail to other recipients, assess the situation and see whether the recipient in the cc field needs to know your response, otherwise they will not know whether they have to act on your message.

Conclusion

Just as you read a conventional letter before putting it in the envelope, read your e-mail carefully before hitting the 'send' button because once you have done it you won't get a second chance to recall it; this is all the more important for forwarded mails and blind carbon copies. Make doubly sure that your mail does not reach unintended recipients. As mentioned earlier, do not send confidential or sensitive matter either within the text or as attachments. Even if you delete the mail, computers have residual memories and data can be stored and passed on.

As a professional, take a look at your e-mail address. What does it say about you? For Do you think it will impress your prospective employer or business acquaintance? It is a good idea to use your initials and your last name. A formal address should be kept for business purposes. Many organisations on the other hand provide their employees with personalised e-mail addresses.

Following the points mentioned here will help you to write correct and effective e-mails.

ASSIGNMENT

1. What are advantages of e-mails over conventional forms of correspondence?
2. Briefly describe the structure of an e-mail.
3. Mention some of the kinds of e-mails that are used for business correspondence.
4. Why do you think it is important to follow e-mail etiquette? Give your answer in about 100 words.